GITA FOR

Shivam Dubey, Nandini Mundada
and Nidhi Garg

Chapter 11: Understanding Dharma

Anant: Kapil, what is "dharma"? I hear that word a lot, but I don't really understand what it means.

Kapil: That's a great question, Anant! Dharma is a little word with a very big meaning. It's like a guide that helps us understand what the right thing to do is in any situation.

Anant: So, it's like rules we have to follow?

Kapil: Kind of, but it's more than just rules. Dharma is about doing what's right, not because someone told you to, but because it's the best thing for everyone, including yourself. Imagine you're playing a game. There are rules to make sure the game is fair, right?

Anant: Yes, if everyone cheats, the game isn't fun.

Kapil: Exactly! Dharma is like those rules, but for life. It helps us make choices that are good and fair, not just for ourselves, but for others too. It's about being kind, honest, and responsible, no matter what.

Anant: What if I make a mistake?

Kapil: That's okay, Anant. Mistakes are part of learning. As long as you're trying your best to follow your dharma, you're doing the right thing. Dharma isn't about being perfect—it's about doing your best to make good choices and help others.

Anant: So, as long as I try to be fair and do the right thing, I'm following my dharma?

Kapil: Exactly! And here's another important part: dharma can change. As you grow up and your responsibilities change, so does your dharma. The dharma of a child is to learn, and the dharma of a parent is to care for their family. It's all about finding balance and doing what's needed in the moment.

Anant: That sounds really important!

Kapil: It is! Following your dharma helps you live a happy and meaningful life. When everyone follows their dharma, it's like all the pieces of a puzzle fitting together to make the world a better place.

Anant: That's really interesting. But what about people who do different kinds of work? Like doctors, farmers, or teachers?

Kapil: That brings us to another important concept, Varna. The ancient system divided people into different groups, called varnas, to help them find their dharma. Think of it like different teams in a big game. Each team has a special role, and when everyone plays their part, the game goes smoothly.

Anant: So, are Varna like teams?

Kapil: Exactly! There are four main Varnas, or teams, in this big game of life. The first one is called the Brahmins. They are like the teachers and priests. They study and share knowledge, and they help others understand what is right and good.

Anant: So they're like our school teachers?

Kapil: Yes, very much like that! The next team is the Kshatriyas. They are the protectors and leaders, like the heroes in our stories who fight for justice and protect the people. They make sure that everyone is safe and that the rules are fair.

Anant: Like kings and soldiers?

Kapil: That's right! The third team is the Vaishyas. They are the traders, farmers, and businesspeople. They make sure that there is food to eat, clothes to wear, and everything else that people need. They're like the people who run shops and farms.

Did You Know?

The Bhagavad Gita has been translated into over 75 languages worldwide, including more than 300 translations in English alone.

MCQ

What is the basic meaning of 'dharma'?
a) A set of strict rules to follow
b) Doing what is right, not because someone told you to, but because it's the best thing for everyone
c) A way to win a game
d) Only something religious people follow

What happens if someone makes a mistake while following their dharma?
a) They are punished
b) Mistakes are part of learning, and trying one's best is what matters
c) They can no longer follow their dharma
d) They must follow someone else's dharma

Answers: B, B

Anant: So they take care of the things we need every day?

Kapil: Exactly, Anant! The last team is the Shudras. They are the helpers and supporters. They do many important tasks that keep everything running smoothly, like building things, cleaning, and helping in different kinds of work. Without them, nothing would get done properly.

Anant: So everyone has an important job?

Kapil: Yes, and that's the key. Every Varna, or team, is important, and each person's role is valuable. But here's something very important to remember:

Anant: What's that?

Kapil: In the past, some people thought you had to stay in the Varna you were born into, but that's not true. You can choose your own path based on what you're good at and what makes you happy. A family might have members in different Varnas, doing different things, and that's perfectly fine.

Anant: So, I can choose what I want to do when I grow up?

Kapil: Absolutely! You can choose what feels right for you. The idea of Varna is about finding the best way to use your talents to help others and make the world a better place. It's not about where you're born or what others expect you to do. You are free to choose your own path!

Anant: That's good to know! So, it's about what we do, not just where we come from?

Kapil: Exactly, Anant. It's all about doing your best, helping others, and finding joy in what you do. That's the real spirit of Varna!
But here's something very important—everyone's dharma is different, and it's better to do your own dharma, even if it's not perfect, than to try and do someone else's dharma.

Anant: So, even if someone is not perfect at what they do, they should still do what they are meant to do?

Kapil: Yes! For example, imagine you are really good at drawing, but your friend is good at sports. If you try to do what your friend does, you might not be as happy or successful because it's not your true path. It's better to focus on what you are good at and what makes you happy.

Anant: But Kapil, isn't it unfair to say some jobs are more important than others?

Kapil: You're right to think about fairness, Anant. The idea of varna was never meant to make one person better than another. It's about understanding that everyone has a special role, and all roles are important.

Unfortunately, over time, some people misunderstood this idea and started thinking that some roles were more important, which led to the caste system being misused. But we should always remember that every person is valuable, no matter what they do.

Anant: That makes sense. Thanks, Kapil! I'm going to think about all of this and try to find what this means for me.

Kapil: That's a great start, Anant. Remember, life is a journey, and each step you take with wisdom and care brings you closer to true happiness and understanding.

Mantra:

"Om Tat Sat"
It signifies the connection of everything in the universe and the higher reality beyond what we see. It aligns us with ultimate truth and the divine, reminding us to live in harmony with this understanding.

Gyan:

How does dharma change as one grows up?
a) Dharma stays the same throughout life
b) Dharma is only important for adults
c) Dharma changes as responsibilities change with age
d) Dharma applies only to specific roles in society

What is the most important aspect of the concept of 'varna'?
a) You must stay in the varna you are born into
b) Everyone should follow the same varna
c) Some varnas are more important than others
d) You can choose your path based on your skills and interests

Answers: C, D

Karm: Draw Your Varna

Draw yourself in a role or job you feel connected to—whether it's being a teacher, leader, helper, or anything else. Then, write down how you believe your role contributes to the community and helps others.

Chapter 12: Key Concepts from the Gita

Anant: Kapil, I've been learning a lot from our talks. But I still have some questions about the things Lord Krishna said in the Gita. Can we go over some of them?

Kapil: Of course, Anant! What would you like to discuss?

Anant: We have talked about how our actions are important. But I was thinking, why do our lives change so much from when we are born to when we die? Why do people live different kinds of lives?

Kapil: That's a good question, Anant. You see, life is like a journey that has different stages. In the Gita, we are taught that human life is divided into four stages, called ashramas.

Anant: Four stages? What are they?

Kapil: The first stage is called Brahmacharya. Brahmacharya is pronounced as "Brah-ma-char-ya." It's the time when a person is young and is a student, like us. This is when you learn new things and prepare for the future.

Anant: Oh, so it's like going to school and learning everything I need to know?

Kapil: Exactly! The second stage is called Grihastha. Grihastha is pronounced as "Grih-has-tha."

This is when a person grows up, gets married, and starts a family. During this time, people work hard to support their family and contribute to society.

Anant: That sounds like what my parents are doing.

Kapil: Yes, that's right! After this comes the third stage, Vanaprastha. Vanaprastha is pronounced as "Vah-nuh-pras-tha." In this stage, a person gradually withdraws from family life and starts focusing more on spiritual practices, preparing for the next stage.

Anant: So, they start living more simply?

Kapil: Yes, and the final stage is called Sannyasa. Sannyasa is pronounced as "Sun-nyah-sah." This is when a person renounces all worldly attachments and dedicates themselves fully to spiritual life, seeking to understand the deeper meaning of life and the universe.

Anant: Kapil, you mentioned earlier how people in Sannyasa let go of all attachments to focus on spiritual life. Does that mean they've also accepted that everything in the world is always changing? Is it really true that everything changes all the time?

Did You Know?

The Nile River, the longest in the world, has changed its path for millions of years due to natural forces, showing that rivers are never the same.

Kapil: Our bodies are changing. Our minds are changing. The world is changing. Everything in nature is constantly changing, even if the change is very slow. Even the universe is constantly changing.

Anant: I don't think so. The river is not changing. The rocks are not changing.

Kapil: They are, all the time. From the time a river forms and starts flowing, so much in it would have changed when you see it now. Rivers are impacted by activity from other forms of nature. When you dip your toe in a river, the mud from your toes is now in that water. So some change has taken place. It is not exactly the same as it was.

Similarly, for a rock. Over hundreds and thousands of years, the surface of the rock changes. The cells that make up the rock are changing. The rocks on a trekking path become smoother after many, many years because of so many people having walked on them. We might not be able to see all the change that is happening, but it is happening all the time.

MCQ

What is the first stage of life according to the Gita?

a) Grihastha

b) Vanaprastha

c) Sannyasa

d) Brahmacharya

What does the Grihastha stage primarily focus on?

a) Learning new things

b) Raising a family and contributing to society

c) Focusing on spiritual practices

d) Renouncing worldly attachments

In the Vanaprastha stage, what does a person start to focus on?

a) Working hard for their family

b) Learning and education

c) Gradually withdrawing from family life and focusing on spirituality

d) Taking up leadership roles

Answers: D, B, C

Anant: Then is there nothing that does not change?

Kapil: There is one thing that does not change. It is the Atman. While all other things in the universe are born and die, the Atman cannot be destroyed. We also call it Brahman. The entire universe has originated from Brahman.

The same Atman is in all of us. This means that in spite of our differences, we are all one. It teaches us that we should treat everyone with love, respect, and compassion. We do not differentiate between people based on their color, religion, nationality, or wealth. Our spiritual texts teach us that inside all of us is the same Atman. We should always keep that in mind when we are dealing with other people.

Anant: What about when people do bad things?

Kapil: When people do bad things, it is because they have not understood the true meaning of our lives. They think that there is nothing after this life and they want to do anything to make this life comfortable for them. Even when people around us can sometimes be nasty, we should remember that there is the Atman inside of them too. They are just not aware of it.

People who do bad things are often caught up in their desires or fears. They forget the deeper truth—that we are all connected by the Atman. But that doesn't mean we allow others to hurt us. We can be kind and compassionate while still standing up for what is right. Sometimes, showing kindness and understanding can help them realize the truth as well.

Anant: So, even if someone is mean, I should still treat them with respect?

Kapil: Yes, Anant. Treat them with respect, but also protect yourself. You don't have to agree with what they do, but you can choose not to react with anger or hate. By understanding that their Atman is the same as yours, you rise above anger and hatred. It's like a candle lighting another candle—your kindness and understanding can help others see the light.

Anant: I think I get it. So, no matter how things change or what others do, the Atman inside all of us stays the same. That's what makes us all connected!

Kapil: Exactly! And when we live with this understanding, we help the world become a better place. The more people realize the unchanging truth of the Atman, the more love and peace there will be in the world. It all starts with how we treat ourselves and others—by remembering that we are all part of the same greater whole.

Mantra:

Tat Tvam Asi

Meaning: You are That

"Tat Tvam Asi" is a way of saying that the true essence of who you are (your soul, or Atman) is the same as the essence of the entire universe (Brahman). It's like saying that deep inside, you are connected to everything around you because you share the same divine essence.

Gyan:

What is the final stage of human life according to the Gita?

a) Brahmacharya

b) Sannyasa

c) Vanaprastha

d) Grihastha

What is the only thing that does not change according to the Gita?

a) Nature

b) Human desires

c) The Atman (or Brahman)

d) The physical body

Answers: B, C

Karm: Change Timeline:

Create a timeline of your life so far, marking all the major changes you've experienced. Think about moments like moving to a new school, learning a new skill, or making new friends. As you work on your timeline, take some time to reflect on how each change has helped you grow and shaped who you are today.

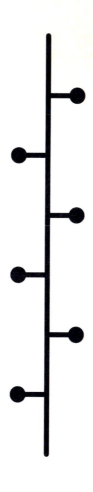

Chapter 13: The Six Enemies

Anant: Kapil, you always leave me with so much to think about. There are a few questions that I have. If you have some time, can I share them with you?

Kapil: Of course, Anant. Tell me - what's on your mind?

Anant: Is it possible that sometimes we have to face challenges or bad feelings? What should we do then?

Kapil: Yes, Anant, life will definitely bring challenges. And sometimes, it's not just the outside problems but also feelings inside us that can become difficult to handle. There are six things that can become our enemies if we're not careful. These are called kama (desire), krodha (anger), lobha (greed), moha (attachment), mada (pride), and matsarya (jealousy).

Anant: Those sound like pretty bad things!

Kapil: They can be bad, Anant, but only if we let them control us. Let's think about each one:

- Kama is desire, wanting something too much. It's okay to have wishes and dreams, but when you want something so badly that it makes you unhappy or causes you to hurt others to get it, then it becomes dangerous. For example, imagine someone who wants a toy so badly that they stop caring about anything else and are willing to fight or lie for it. That's when desire turns into an enemy.

- Krodha is anger. We all feel angry sometimes, but if we let anger take over, it can make us say or do things that hurt others. Imagine losing a game and getting so mad that you yell at your friends or break something. That's when anger becomes a problem.

- Lobha is greed, always wanting more and never feeling satisfied. It's like someone who has plenty but still keeps asking for more, even if it means others get less. Greed makes us forget to share and be kind.

- Moha is attachment, being too attached to things or people. Of course, it's natural to love people and enjoy our things, but sometimes we can become so attached that we become scared of losing them. When that happens, we stop enjoying life and start worrying too much.

- Mada is pride. It's okay to feel proud when we do something good, but if we think we are better than others, it can hurt our relationships. People who are too proud don't listen to others or help those in need.

MCQ

What does 'Kama' refer to in the discussion?

a) Greed

b) Anger

c) Pride

d) Desire

How is 'Krodha' described?

a) The desire to achieve something

b) Anger that can hurt others if not controlled

c) Pride in one's accomplishments

d) Attachment to material things

What does 'Lobha' refer to?

a) Greed, wanting more than needed

b) Jealousy of others' success

c) Anger that cannot be controlled

d) Pride in oneself

Answers: D, B, A

- Matsarya is jealousy. It's when we feel bad because someone else has something that we don't. Instead of being happy for them, jealousy makes us feel unhappy and sometimes even mean.

Anant: Wow! Those really do sound like big obstacles. What can we do to stop them from taking over?

Kapil: The key is to recognize when these feelings arise and not let them take control of us. You can think of it like being a captain of a ship. Imagine you're sailing on a calm sea, but suddenly a big wave of anger or jealousy appears. If you panic and let the wave push you around, you'll lose control of your ship. But if you stay calm and steer carefully, you can navigate through the storm.

One way to stay in control is by practicing dharma—doing what is right, even when it's hard. Dharma is like the compass that helps you steer your ship. If you always follow your dharma, you can make good decisions, even when things get tough.

Anant: But how do I stay calm when I feel angry or jealous?

Kapil: It's not always easy, but there are ways to handle these feelings. One way is through meditation and mindfulness. If you take a moment to breathe and calm your mind when you feel anger or jealousy coming, it gives you time to think and make a better choice. It's like stepping away from a game to take a deep breath before jumping back in.

Another way is to remember that everyone has these feelings. You're not alone in feeling angry or wanting something. But instead of letting those feelings control you, you can learn to understand them and respond wisely. Just like in a game, even if you lose or things don't go as planned, you can still play fairly and kindly.

Anant: So, if I control these enemies, I can stay on the right path?

Kapil: Exactly! If you can learn to control your desires, anger, greed, attachment, pride, and jealousy, you will be much stronger. You'll make better choices, treat others kindly, and stay focused on your goals. Life is full of challenges, but with practice, you can always steer your ship in the right direction. By controlling these enemies, you become the master of your own mind and actions.

Anant: That sounds like something I want to do!

Kapil: You're already on the right track, Anant. Just remember, every day is a chance to practice. The more you pay attention to your feelings and make wise choices, the better you'll become at facing life's challenges with strength and kindness.

Did You Know?

When we experience desire, the brain releases dopamine, a chemical that makes us feel pleasure. This can motivate us to achieve our goals, but it can also lead to unhealthy cravings if not managed.

Mantra:

Sarvam khalu idam Brahma

Meaning: "Everything here is indeed Brahman."

Gyan:

What happens when someone has too much 'Moha' (attachment)?

a) They forget to share

b) They become fearful of losing things or people

c) They hurt others to get what they want

d) They become proud of themselves

What is 'Mada' and why can it be harmful?

a) Pride that makes a person believe they are better than others

b) Greed that makes people take from others

c) Anger that causes people to break things

d) Desire that makes people unhappy

Answers: B, A

Karm: Star Breathing

Chapter 14: The Five Koshas

Anant: Kapil, last time you spoke to me about the six enemies—desire, anger, greed, attachment, pride, and jealousy. You also shared some ways in which we can keep these enemies away. I would like you to help me a little bit more on how we can work on ourselves to do that.

Kapil: Good question, Anant! It all starts with understanding our inner self. Our true self, or Atman, is covered by different layers, like how an onion has layers. These layers are called koshas, and there are five of them. Each kosha is like a part of us that we need to understand and take care of.

Anant: Five koshas? That sounds like a lot! What are they?

Kapil: Don't worry, I'll explain it simply. Think of these koshas as layers of yourself, each one playing an important role. Let's go through them one by one.

Physical Body (Annamaya Kosha): This is the easiest to understand because it's your body—your arms, legs, head, and everything you can see. It's like the outermost layer, like a jacket you wear. Just like you need to keep your body healthy with good food, exercise, and sleep, this layer needs regular care.

- Energy Body (Pranamaya Kosha): Inside the physical body is the energy that keeps you alive. This energy helps you breathe, move, and feel active, like the battery in a toy or the engine in a car. When you feel tired or full of energy, it's because of this layer. Doing things like deep breathing or yoga can help keep this energy strong.

- Mind (Manomaya Kosha): This layer is about your thoughts, feelings, and imagination. It's like a control room that decides what you think and how you feel. Sometimes your mind can be busy, like a monkey jumping from tree to tree. But with practice, you can train it to be calm. This is why meditation or focusing on something you enjoy, like reading or drawing, is helpful—it quiets your mind.

- Wisdom Body (Vijnanamaya Kosha): This layer is the wisdom inside you that helps you make smart decisions. It's like a wise teacher in your head, guiding you to do the right thing. When you learn something new or when you figure out a good way to solve a problem, you're using this layer.

- Blissful Body (Anandamaya Kosha): The last layer is all about joy and happiness, the kind of happiness that comes from deep inside. When everything is going well and you feel at peace with yourself and the world around you, this layer is shining the brightest. It's like the warmth you feel on a sunny day or the joy you get when you do something you really love.

Gyan: Match the following

Column A (Koshas)

1. Annamaya Kosha
2. Pranamaya Kosha
3. Manomaya Kosha
4. Vijnanamaya Kosha
5. Anandamaya Kosha

Column B (Description)

A. Layer representing joy and inner happiness
B. Layer responsible for thoughts and feelings
C. The physical body that needs care and nourishment
D. The energy body that fuels our actions
E. The layer of wisdom guiding our decisions

Answers

Annamaya Kosha - C. The physical body that needs care and nourishment

Pranamaya Kosha - D. The energy body that fuels our actions

Manomaya Kosha - B. Layer responsible for thoughts and feelings

Vijnanamaya Kosha - E. The layer of wisdom guiding our decisions

Anandamaya Kosha - A. Layer representing joy and inner happiness

Anant: Wow, that's pretty amazing! So, are these koshas like layers of clothing we wear?

Kapil: Exactly! You could think of the koshas as layers of clothing that protect the Atman, your true self. The physical body is the thickest, most visible layer, while bliss is the deepest, closest to your Atman.

Anant: So what do these layers do? And why do we have to take care of them?

Kapil: These layers protect and support your true self. If one layer isn't cared for properly, it affects all the others. Think of it like a garden. The physical body is the soil, the energy body is the sunlight, the mind is the water, wisdom is the fertilizer, and bliss is the beautiful flowers that bloom when everything is in harmony.

If you only water the garden and don't give it sunlight, the plants won't grow strong. In the same way, if you only take care of your physical body and don't pay attention to your energy or mind, you won't feel balanced or happy. By taking care of all five koshas, you can live a more peaceful and joyful life.

Anant: So if I work on all these layers, will it help me handle bad feelings like anger and jealousy?

Kapil: Absolutely! When you take care of each kosha, you become stronger, like a tree with deep roots.

The six enemies—desire, anger, greed, attachment, pride, and jealousy—are like strong winds that try to knock the tree over. But if the tree has deep roots, it can stand tall, even in a storm. The koshas are your roots, and by caring for them, you make sure you stay balanced, no matter what challenges life brings.

Anant: I get it now! So if I take care of my body, energy, mind, wisdom, and happiness, I can be strong like a tree, and those bad feelings won't knock me over.

Kapil: Exactly, Anant! And remember, this is a lifelong journey. Just like a tree doesn't grow overnight, we keep working on our koshas every day. When you're mindful of all the layers inside you, you can stay true to your dharma—your life's purpose—and live with peace, strength, and joy.
You'll also notice, Anant, that as you grow and start paying attention to these koshas, you'll get better at understanding your own feelings and what's happening around you. Sometimes, when things don't go the way we want, we feel upset or frustrated, but by taking care of these layers, you'll feel more in control. For example, when you know your mind is getting upset, you can take a deep breath, quiet your energy, and make a better choice.

Anant: That sounds helpful! So, it's like I can control myself better by working on these koshas?

Kapil: Yes, exactly! And as you keep working on them, you'll also feel more connected to others, because everyone has these koshas. It teaches us to be kind and patient with others because they're working on themselves too.

Mantra:

Gurubrahma Guruvishnu Gurudevo Maheshvara,

Gurusasakshat Param Brahma Tasmai Sri Guruve Namah

This mantra is about showing great respect and love for the Guru, or teacher, who helps us learn important lessons in life. It says the Guru is like Brahma, the creator, who helps us start learning; like Vishnu, the one who protects, who helps us keep growing; and like Shiva, who helps us let go of things we don't need anymore.

Gyan:

Why is it important to take care of all five koshas?

A) To impress others

B) To protect the Atman and maintain balance

C) To achieve wealth

D) To become famous

What is the overall purpose of understanding and caring for the koshas?

A) To win competitions

B) To stay true to one's dharma and live a balanced life

C) To gain material possessions

D) To avoid all challenges

Answers: B, B

Karm: Energy Reflection Chart

Create a chart tracking energy levels throughout the day for one week. Note when you feel most energized and when you feel drained, linking these to activities and foods.

DAY 1

DAY 2

DAY 3

DAY 4

DAY 5

DAY 6

DAY 7

Chapter 15: Overcoming Attachment, Fear, and Anger

Anant: Lord Krishna also talks about overcoming attachment, fear, and anger. How can we do that?

Kapil: You're right, Anant. Krishna says these three—attachment, fear, and anger—are like big, heavy blocks that stop us from finding true happiness. They are things we all face, but there are ways we can work on them to live better and happier lives.

Let's start with attachment. Attachment means holding on too tightly to things or people, thinking that without them, we can't be happy. But the truth is, everything around us keeps changing. We grow older, seasons change, and even our favorite toys can break. If we get too attached to things, we can feel really sad when they go away or change. Instead, we can enjoy things and the people in our lives while remembering that it's okay if they aren't with us forever. Our happiness shouldn't depend only on what we have or who is around us.

Think of it like holding sand in your hand. If you grip it too tightly, the sand slips through your fingers. But if you hold it gently, the sand stays. That's how we should think about attachment—enjoy things but don't hold on too tightly. When we let go a little, we can feel much more relaxed and peaceful.

Now let's talk about fear. Fear can be like a shadow that makes things seem scarier than they are. Most of our fears are in our minds. Sometimes we are afraid of things that haven't even happened yet, or we worry about things that might never happen. When we trust ourselves, and remember that Krishna is with us, it gives us the courage to face our fears. Imagine you're scared of the dark. But when you turn on the light, you realize there's nothing there to be afraid of. It's the same with fear. When we shine the light of courage on it, we often find that what we feared wasn't as big or scary as we thought.

To overcome fear, we need to take small steps. If we're afraid of speaking in front of people, we can start by speaking in front of just one friend or family member. By facing our fears little by little, they become smaller, and we become stronger.

Finally, let's look at anger. When we feel anger, it's like a fire that burns inside us. If we don't control it, it can make us say or do things we regret. Anger can also hurt others and damage our relationships. But, just like putting out a fire, we can calm down our anger by taking a deep breath and thinking before we act.

Imagine you're holding a glass of water and someone bumps into you. If you're calm, the water might spill just a little, and you can clean it up. But if you're angry and shake the glass, the water spills everywhere, making a bigger mess. When we control our anger, we keep the mess small and manageable. Krishna teaches us that by staying calm and patient, even when things upset us, we can handle situations much better.

Did you know:

The brain can change and adapt through neuroplasticity. Practicing mindfulness and emotional regulation techniques can physically reshape neural pathways, helping us respond to attachment, fear, and anger more effectively.

MCQ

What are the three emotions that can prevent true happiness?

A) Happiness, sadness, and joy

B) Attachment, fear, and anger

C) Love, fear, and excitement

D) Jealousy, greed, and pride

How should we approach attachment to things or people?

A) Hold on tightly to everything

B) Let go completely of all attachments

C) Enjoy things while remembering they can change

D) Avoid forming attachments altogether

Answers: B, C

Anant: That makes sense. So, it's important not to let anger control us.

Kapil: Exactly! When we let go of attachment, face our fears with courage, and manage our anger, we become more peaceful and balanced. Krishna says that when we focus on what's good and true—on him, on being kind and doing the right things—we can find lasting happiness. This doesn't mean we won't ever feel these emotions, but we learn not to let them control us.

When we can overcome attachment, fear, and anger, it's like clearing the path to joy. It's not always easy, but with practice and by remembering Krishna's teachings, we can all learn to live with more peace and happiness in our hearts.

Anant: This reminds me of the words "raga" and "dvesha." I think these words are also connected somehow to what you just spoke. Can you explain to them what they mean?

Kapil: That's a great question! These two are connected to attachment and dislike, and they can affect how we act if we're not careful. **Raga** means attachment or a strong liking for something, like when you really love a particular toy or snack. **Dvesha** is the opposite—it's when you strongly dislike something, like a food you don't enjoy or a task you don't want to do.

Anant: So, it's like liking or disliking things?

Kapil: Yes, but it goes deeper. Sometimes, our attachment to things we like, or our dislike for things, can control how we act. For example, if you're too attached to your favorite toy, you might feel upset or angry if you lose it or if someone else plays with it. Or if there's a chore you don't like, dvesha might make you avoid it, even if it's important to do.

Anant: So, it's important to not let these feelings take over?

Kapil: Exactly! It's natural to like or dislike things, but when we let these feelings control us, we end up reacting without thinking. It's like being a puppet pulled by strings. If we're too attached to something or too full of dislike, it's harder to make smart, balanced choices. Krishna teaches us to stay in control of our emotions and actions. We can still enjoy things without getting too attached, and we can handle things we don't like without getting overwhelmed.

Anant: So, the key is balance?

Kapil: That's right. When we don't let raga and dvesha control us, we stay balanced and can make wiser decisions. Overcoming these feelings helps us live a more peaceful life and keeps us focused on our dharma, our true purpose.

Mantra:

Ekam Sat Vipra Bahudha Vadanti

This is a shloka that teaches us something important about truth. The saying tells us that "There is only one truth, but wise people describe it in many different ways."

Gyan:

What do "raga" and "dvesha" refer to?

A) Attachment and freedom

B) Attachment and dislike

C) Happiness and sadness

D) Trust and fear

What is the main lesson about emotions in this context?

A) Emotions should be avoided at all costs

B) It's okay to let emotions control actions

C) We should not let emotions control us

D) Only positive emotions matter

Answers: B, C

Karm: Facing Fears

Identify one small fear you have (e.g., public speaking, trying a new activity). Over the course of a week, take one small action toward confronting that fear (e.g., speak in front of one friend, try the new activity once). Reflect on how you felt afterward and what you learned.

○ ....
○ ....
○ ....
○ ....
○ ....
○ ....
○ ....
○ ....
○ ....
○ ....
○ ....
○ ....

Chapter 16: Finding Balance: The Right Way to Act and Let Go

Anant: Kapil, I've been wondering—what is better: the Yoga of Action, where we do our duties, or the Yoga of Renunciation, where we give up actions and focus on meditation?

Kapil: That's a great question, Anant. Both paths are important, but Krishna says that the Yoga of Action is higher.

Anant: Why is that? Isn't sitting in meditation and focusing on inner peace more important?

Kapil: Meditation is definitely valuable, but think of it this way: If someone near you is in trouble, what's more helpful—sitting quietly and meditating, or going and helping them?

Anant: I guess helping them would be more important.

Kapil: Exactly! The Yoga of Action means doing your duty, helping others, and making the world a better place. Imagine if a firefighter only sat and meditated while a house was on fire. The right thing to do in that moment would be to take action, to help people in need. That's why Krishna says the Yoga of Action is more important. We should never ignore our duties or the people around us.

Anant: So, does that mean we should always be doing things and never meditate?

Kapil: Not at all! Meditation helps us focus and keep our minds calm, but it should not be used as an excuse to avoid responsibility. Balance is key. We need both—times of action and times of quiet reflection. But when it comes to what is more important in the world, helping others through action comes first.

Anant: Kapil, I've also been thinking about something else. Sometimes I look at people who seem so talented or kind, and I feel like I'm not as good as them. What should I do when I feel like that?

Kapil: It's natural to admire others, but remember, Anant, you should never put yourself down while respecting someone else. Each of us has our own unique talents and strengths. Just because someone is good at one thing doesn't mean you aren't good at something else. Think of it like this—if you were a flower, you wouldn't compare yourself to a tree. You both have different purposes, and both are important.

Anant: So, we should respect others but not feel bad about ourselves?
Kapil: Yes, exactly! We should respect others for their talents and strengths, but also respect ourselves. Everyone has something special to offer, including you.

Did You Know?

Neurotransmitters like serotonin and dopamine play crucial roles in mood regulation. Engaging in actions that contribute to others' well-being can boost these chemicals, promoting happiness and emotional stability.

MCQ

What does the Yoga of Action focus on?
a) Only meditating
b) Fulfilling one's duties and helping others
c) Renouncing all actions
d) Avoiding responsibilities

According to the conversation, how should meditation be used?
a) As a way to avoid responsibilities
b) As an excuse to not act
c) To focus and calm the mind while balancing responsibilities
d) Only during difficult times

Answers: B, C

Kapil: Challenges and distractions are actually good for us. Think of your mind like a muscle. How do we make our muscles stronger?

Anant: By exercising them.

Kapil: Right! And how do we exercise them? By lifting weights or using resistance. It's the same with the mind. If there were no challenges, no distractions, your mind wouldn't have a chance to grow stronger. It's in the midst of challenges that we strengthen our minds. When you face a tough situation, it's like lifting weights for your brain. The more you practice staying calm and focused during difficult times, the stronger your mind becomes.

Anant: I get that. But what about attachment? Krishna often talks about not being too attached to things. Should we just give up on everything?

Kapil: That's a common misunderstanding. Krishna doesn't mean you should give up everything. Complete freedom, as Krishna explains, comes when we can both attach and detach as needed.

Anant: What does that mean?

Kapil: Let's say you really love your pet. That's attachment. It's fine to love your pet, but if one day your pet gets sick or passes away, you shouldn't let that destroy your happiness. You need to have the ability to detach from that attachment when necessary. It's about balance

Anant: So, being free doesn't mean not caring about anything?

Kapil: Exactly! Freedom means you have the ability to care deeply and form attachments, but you also have the strength to let go when the time comes. If you can only attach but can't let go, you're not truly free. And if you can only detach but never form connections, that's not freedom either.

Anant: So freedom is about having the choice to do both?

Kapil: Yes. Imagine a bird with only one wing. It wouldn't be able to fly. To truly soar, it needs both wings—just like we need both the ability to attach and the ability to detach. When you can do both, you experience real freedom and balance in life.

Anant: That makes sense, Kapil. I think I'm starting to understand why Krishna talks about all these different paths. It's not about just doing one thing, like only meditating or only acting. It's about learning how to live in balance with everything.

Kapil: Exactly, Anant. Life is full of different paths, and it's important to walk them with awareness, understanding that balance is the key. By learning to act with purpose, to respect both ourselves and others, and by strengthening our minds through challenges, we can live a life that is both peaceful and meaningful.

Mantra:

Satyam Jnaanam Anantam Brahma

The mantra "Satyam Jnaanam Anantam Brahma" describes the nature of Brahman, or the ultimate reality, in three ways:

- Satyam means truth. Brahman is the eternal truth that never changes. It is the foundation of all that exists.
- Jnaanam means knowledge. Brahman is pure knowledge and awareness. It is the source of all wisdom and understanding.
- Anantam means infinite. Brahman is limitless, without any boundaries in time, space, or form. It is beyond what we can measure or see.

So, this mantra tells us that Brahman, or the ultimate reality, is the eternal truth, the source of all knowledge, and infinite in nature.

Gyan:

What should one do when feeling inferior to someone else's talents?

a) Admire them and give up

b) Disregard their talents

c) Respect their talents while recognizing your own strengths

d) Compare yourself constantly to them

Answer: C

Karm: Attachment vs. Detachment Exercise

In the Attachment vs. Detachment Exercise, choose a favorite item, like a toy or book, and write about why you love it. Then, imagine how you would feel if you had to let it go. This exercise helps you explore the balance between attachment and detachment.

Chapter 17: The Yoga of Balance

Anant: Kapil, you've talked before about seeing everyone as equal. Is that something we can all learn?

Kapil: Yes, Anant. It's called "samatva," which means a sense of equality. But it's not something that just happens overnight. We need training for it, and one of the best trainings is meditation.

Anant: How does meditation help us with that?

Kapil: Meditation helps quiet the mind. When the mind is calm, we can see things more clearly and not get too affected by what we like or don't like. For example, if someone says something that usually makes you angry, with meditation, you might not get as upset. You start to see everyone—friends, family, even people you don't get along with—as equal.

Anant: So, you can learn to stay calm?

Kapil: Exactly! It's about being steady, no matter if things are going well or not. That's what samatva is all about—keeping a balanced mind whether life brings good times or challenges.

Anant: What about desires? I sometimes feel like I always want more, and it makes me frustrated when I don't get it.

Kapil: That's normal. We all have desires. But the problem is when we can't control them. When we chase one thing, and then as soon as we get it, we want the next thing. It's like running on a never-ending treadmill. This is how desires make us slaves. When we're constantly running after things, we'll never be fully satisfied.

Anant: So how do we stop chasing desires?

Kapil: The key is to focus on something higher. Instead of putting all our energy into getting more toys or achievements, we can use that energy for spiritual growth. Think about improving your inner self, practicing kindness, and finding peace within. When we do that, we feel fulfilled from the inside, not by the things around us.

Anant: That makes sense. So, we have to control our own minds.

Kapil: Exactly! There's a teaching in the Gita that says, "Raise yourself by yourself. Don't let yourself down, for you alone are your own friend, and you alone are your own enemy." It means that we are responsible for our own growth and happiness. It reminds us that we have the power to improve ourselves and make good choices. If we stay positive, work hard, and learn from mistakes, we become our best friend by helping ourselves succeed.
On the other hand, if we let negative thoughts or bad habits control us, we can become our own enemy, holding ourselves back. This teaches us that instead of blaming others, we should take responsibility for our actions and choices, because we have the ability to shape our own future.

Did you know?

Studies indicate that adopting a growth mindset—believing that abilities can improve through effort—can lead to increased motivation and resilience. This relates to taking responsibility for personal growth, as highlighted in Kapil's teachings.

MCQ

What does "samatva" mean?
A) Equality
B) Meditation
C) Happiness
D) Anger

What should be the focus instead of chasing desires?
A) Getting more toys
B) Improving our inner self
C) Achieving fame
D) Competing with others

Answers: A, B

Anant: So, it's about taking responsibility for ourselves?

Kapil: Yes, that's the most important part. We have the ability to control how we react to things. If we blame others or don't take responsibility, we can't improve. But if we understand that we are in control of our actions and thoughts, we can grow stronger.

Anant: But it's hard to always stay balanced. What if someone is really mean or unfair?

Kapil: It can be difficult, but a person who can stay calm and equal-minded in all situations is someone who has mastered yoga. Yoga isn't just about exercises or meditation. It's also about how we treat others. Imagine being able to see everyone—whether they are friends, enemies, or strangers—with the same respect and kindness. That's real success in yoga.

Anant: So, even if someone is mean, we should still see them with kindness?

Kapil: Yes. People who are equal-minded look at well-wishers, friends, enemies, relatives, and strangers with the same kindness and fairness. They understand that everyone is going through their own challenges, and they don't let anger or frustration get in the way. By staying calm and treating everyone equally, we become stronger inside.

Anant: How can we get better at this?

Kapil: One way is by living in balance. Success in yoga isn't for someone who eats too much or too little, or someone who sleeps too much or barely at all. We need balance in everything—our eating, sleeping, and even our activities. When we are balanced in these areas, we feel better and can focus more on what's important.

Anant: So, it's not good to go to extremes?

Kapil: Exactly. Yoga teaches that moderation is the key. When we are balanced, we are happier and healthier, and yoga becomes the destroyer of unhappiness.

Anant: That sounds like a good way to live. What about how we treat others?

Kapil: A simple rule is: "As you feel about yourself, feel about others, too." If something is painful for you, you should avoid doing it to someone else. Treat others with the same kindness and respect you want for yourself. It's like sharing a toy—you don't want to break someone else's toy, just like you don't want yours to be broken.

Anant: So, we need to see others as we see ourselves?

Kapil: Yes, when we see others with the same care that we have for ourselves, we live in harmony. This is the true essence of yoga—being balanced, taking responsibility for ourselves, and treating others with kindness and fairness. That's the path to real happiness.

Mantra:

OM Namo bhagvate Rudraye

The mantra means, "I bow to Lord Rudra (Shiva)," asking for his blessings to remove obstacles, transform negativity, and bring peace.

Gyan:

What does the teaching from the Gita say about self-responsibility?

A) We should blame others for our problems

B) We are our own friend and enemy

C) We should ignore our thoughts

D) We need help from others to grow

What is the key to living in balance?

A) Being extreme in actions

B) Practicing yoga exercises

C) Moderation in eating, sleeping, and activities

D) Ignoring responsibilities

Answers: B, C

Karm: Gratitude Lists

Write down three things you are grateful for each day for a week.

Chapter 18: The Power of Bhakti and Emotions

Anant: Kapil, you mentioned different types of yoga before, like karma yoga and jnana yoga. What is Bhakti yoga?

Kapil: Good question, Anant! Bhakti yoga is the path of devotion. You see, we have many aspects of our personality, and one of the most important is our emotions. Bhakti yoga helps us handle those emotions in a smart and meaningful way. Instead of letting our emotions control us, Bhakti yoga teaches us to channel them toward love for the divine. It's about forming a deep emotional connection with God or a higher power, and this devotion can bring peace and joy.

Anant: So, it's like using our feelings to get closer to something higher?

Kapil: Exactly! It's about taking the love, devotion, and even the sadness or longing we feel and offering it to the divine. It's not just about feeling love but about directing that love toward something that helps us grow spiritually.

Anant: That sounds beautiful! But sometimes our emotions can be all over the place. How do we manage that?

Kapil: That's the beauty of Bhakti yoga. It teaches us to use our emotions in the right way.

It's like learning to sail a boat—you use the wind (your emotions) to guide you, but you still need to steer with intelligence. When we learn to direct our emotions toward the divine, we grow closer to understanding the truth of the universe.

Anant: Speaking of truth, you once told me about Brahman. Can you explain more about how everything comes from Brahman?

Kapil: Think of it like the ocean. When you see a wave, by the time you recognize it, the wave has already changed. But the truth is, the wave is just part of the ocean—it comes from the ocean, stays for a while, and then goes back into the ocean. Similarly, Brahman is the ultimate reality, the source of everything. The universe, like the wave, comes from Brahman, exists for some time, and then returns to Brahman. Everything you see, hear, and touch is part of this greater reality.

Anant: So, Brahman is like the ocean, and we're all waves?

Kapil: Exactly. Everything in the universe is a part of Brahman. Just like the waves are not separate from the ocean, we and everything around us are not separate from Brahman. When we understand this, we realize that all things are interconnected, and that helps us develop love and compassion for others.

Anant: That makes sense. But what if someone is doing something wrong? How do we handle that without being harsh?

MCQ

What is Bhakti yoga primarily focused on?

A) Physical fitness

B) Devotion and emotional connection to the divine

C) Intellectual discussions

D) Social service

How does Bhakti yoga help us manage our emotions?

A) By suppressing them

B) By channeling them toward love for the divine

C) By encouraging free expression

D) By ignoring them

What are iccha and dvesa?

A) Forms of meditation

B) Types of yoga

C) Emotions related to desire and aversion

D) Stages of spiritual growth

Answers: B, B, C

Anant: So, we get angry because we don't get what we want?

Kapil: Yes, and it's something everyone experiences. Our mind is wired to want things, but the problem is, desires never seem to end. Even when you get what you want, soon enough, a new desire pops up. And when that desire isn't fulfilled, you feel upset or angry all over again. But here's the thing—if we let these feelings control us, we're always reacting. We're always wanting something, then getting frustrated when it doesn't come. It's like chasing shadows.

Anant: Wow, that sounds exhausting. So, what can we do about it?

Kapil: The trick is not to let these feelings carry us away. We have to realize that chasing every desire only leads to more craving and frustration. If we're always running after what we want or getting upset when things don't go our way, we miss the bigger picture of life. Desires are like waves—they come and go. But if we get caught up in every wave, we'll never find peace. To break free, we need to learn to let go, to stop being controlled by these desires and emotions.

Anant: So, the key is to control these desires and emotions, right?

Kapil: Yes! Instead of letting your desires control you, learn to control them. If you keep running after one thing after another, you'll never feel satisfied, because there will always be something new to chase.

But if you focus on something higher—like your spiritual growth, understanding the truth of life, or connecting with the divine—you'll find a deeper happiness, one that's not based on getting or losing things. You'll find peace that lasts.

Anant: It sounds like Bhakti yoga can help with that.

Kapil: Absolutely. Bhakti yoga is all about channeling your emotions, especially love and devotion, in the right way. Instead of being swept away by desires or anger, Bhakti helps us direct those feelings toward something greater, something that brings us closer to peace and understanding. When you offer your emotions to the divine, they don't control you anymore; instead, they guide you toward inner peace and balance.

Did you know?

Mahatma Gandhi often turned to the Gita for inspiration, calling it his "spiritual guide."

Mantra:

Sarvam Brahma Mayam

Sarvam Vasudeva Mayam

Meaning:

Everything is Brahman, everything is Shri Krishna

Gyan:

What happens when desires are not fulfilled?

A) We become content

B) We experience anger and frustration

C) We achieve inner peace

D) We gain clarity

Why is chasing every desire considered exhausting?

A) It leads to constant happiness

B) New desires always arise after fulfilling one

C) It is a simple process

D) It helps in emotional growth

Answer: B, B

Karm: Colour The Image

Colour the central image. Take your time and choose colors that reflect how you feel or how you want to feel.

Chapter 19: The Four Paths to the Divine

Anant: Kapil, you've mentioned so many different ways people can connect with the Divine. But is there a specific path that we're supposed to follow?

Kapil: That's a great question, Anant! There are actually four main paths to achieve the Divine, and they're all different. You can choose the one that suits you best, or even combine them. The first is Bhakti, which is the path of love and devotion. The second is Jnana, the path of knowledge and wisdom. The third is Karma, the path of action and doing good deeds. And finally, there's Dhyana, which is the path of meditation and inner focus.

Anant: Wow! Four paths? Can you tell me a bit more about each of them?

Kapil: Of course. Let's start with Bhakti. This is when you feel deep love and devotion toward the Divine. It's all about trusting that love, surrendering to it, and finding joy in it. People on this path often sing, pray, and think of God with their heart. It's a very emotional and loving way to connect with the Divine.

Anant: So it's all about love?

Kapil: Yes! Now, Jnana is different. It's the path of knowledge. Instead of connecting with emotions, people on this path use their mind to understand the nature of the universe and themselves. They seek wisdom by reading spiritual texts and asking deep questions about life.

Anant: And what about Karma?

Kapil: Karma is the path of action. It's about doing your duties and helping others without expecting rewards. You focus on your actions and make sure they are good and selfless. When you act in this way, you come closer to the Divine through your deeds.

Anant: I like that. And Dhyana?

Kapil: Dhyana is the path of meditation. It's when you sit quietly and look within, calming your mind to find peace and focus. Through meditation, you connect with the Divine by going deeper into yourself, focusing on your true nature, and letting go of distractions.

Anant: So we can choose whichever path feels right for us?

Kapil: Exactly, Anant. Some people may feel more connected to the Divine through love and devotion, while others may find their way through knowledge or selfless action. And for some, meditation brings that peace and understanding. All these paths lead to the same goal: realizing the Divine within and around us.

Anant: You've also talked about strengths before. I remember you said there are three kinds of strengths we have—Buddhi Balam, Bahu Balam, and Atma Balam. Can you explain those again?

MCQ

Which of the following is the path of devotion and love toward the Divine?

a) Jnana Yoga

b) Karma Yoga

c) Bhakti Yoga

d) Dhyana Yoga

What is the primary focus of Jnana Yoga?

a) Love and emotions

b) Knowledge and wisdom

c) Physical strength

d) Meditation

What does Karma Yoga emphasize?

a) Meditation and focus

b) Selfless action and duty

c) Gaining spiritual knowledge

d) Devotion and prayer

Answer: C, B, B

Kapil: Sure, let's break them down. Buddhi Balam is the strength of your mind and intellect. This is your ability to think, to make good decisions, and to understand the world around you. It's like having a strong, sharp mind that helps you figure things out.

Anant: So it's like being smart?

Kapil: Exactly! When you have strong Buddhi Balam, you can solve problems, learn new things, and make wise choices. Then we have Bahu Balam, which is the strength of your body—your physical strength. This is important for staying healthy, active, and able to take on challenges in the world.
Anant: Like having muscles and being fit?

Kapil: Yes, it's all about taking care of your body so it stays strong and healthy. But the third strength, Atma Balam, is the most special. It's the strength of your spirit, your inner self. This is what gives you courage, determination, and resilience. It's what helps you stay calm in tough times and face life's challenges with confidence.

Anant: How do we develop that kind of strength?

Kapil: Atma Balam comes from spiritual practice—like meditation, prayer, and living a good, balanced life. When you focus on growing spiritually, you develop a strong inner core that can't be shaken easily.

It's like having an unbreakable spirit that stays steady no matter what happens.

Anant: And what happens when we develop Atma Balam?

Kapil: When you cultivate Atma Balam, you become fearless and peaceful inside. Even if things go wrong around you, you remain calm because you're connected to something deeper. It also helps you treat others with kindness, stay focused on your goals, and not be swayed by distractions. In a way, Atma Balam brings everything together—it supports your mind, body, and soul.

Anant: So, it's important to balance all three strengths?

Kapil: Absolutely. When you have Buddhi Balam, Bahu Balam, and Atma Balam working together, you become a balanced and strong person. You're smart, strong, and spiritually grounded—all at the same time.

Anant: Wow, it sounds like when all three strengths come together, we can really face anything in life! I definitely want to work on building my Atma Balam too.

Did You Know?

Many famous authors and poets, including T.S. Eliot and Carl Jung, have referenced the Gita in their works.

Mantra

Aksaram Brahma Paramam

Meaning: The highest truth, called Brahman, never changes and never goes away. It's always there, like a never-ending light, guiding everything in the universe.

Gyan

Which of the following best describes Dhyana Yoga?
a) Singing and praying to God
b) Reading sacred texts for knowledge
c) Meditating to find inner peace
d) Doing good deeds for others

What is "Buddhi Balam"?
a) Physical strength
b) Strength of the mind and intellect
c) Spiritual strength
d) Emotional strength

Answers: C, B

Karm: Crossword Puzzle

Down

1. Balam The strength of the mind and intellect. (11 letters, two words)

2. Balam The strength of the spirit and inner self. (9 letters, two words)

3. The path of selfless action and doing good deeds without expecting rewards. (5 letters)

4. The path of knowledge and wisdom, seeking the truth. (5 letters)

6. Refers to God or a higher power, the ultimate reality. (6 letters)

8. Balam The strength of the body and physical fitness. (9 letters, two words)

Across

5. A practice of calming the mind and focusing inward. (10 letters)

7. The path of meditation and inner focus. (6 letters)

8. The path of love and devotion to the Divine. (6 letters)

9. Deep knowledge and understanding, especially of spiritual truths. (6 letters)

Chapter 20: Seeing Beyond Appearances

Anant: Kapil, sometimes I wonder how we should treat people who look different or act differently from us. How do we know if someone is good or not just by how they seem?

Kapil: That's a very good question, Anant. One of the most important lessons in life is to not judge people by their appearance. Someone might look simple or ordinary, but they could have a lot of wisdom or goodness inside them. Just because someone doesn't appear impressive doesn't mean they aren't special. It's like finding a beautiful treasure inside a plain box—what's on the outside isn't always what matters most.

Anant: So, we should always look deeper and not make quick judgments?

Kapil: Exactly. We must learn to look beyond what we see on the surface. A person's value is not just in how they look, speak, or act in certain situations. When we learn to see without being influenced by our own likes, dislikes, or attachments, we develop a sakshi bhava, which means the attitude of a witness. A sakshi is someone who watches without getting carried away by emotions or judgments.

Anant: But why do attachments make it hard to see things clearly?

Kapil: Attachments cloud our judgment because they make us see things only from our personal perspective.

For example, if you really like someone, you might overlook their mistakes. Or if you strongly dislike someone, you might only notice the bad things about them. In both cases, you're not seeing the whole truth—you're letting your feelings get in the way. That's why it's important to step back and view things with a calm, clear mind, free from personal attachment. When you develop this ability, you can see the truth of any situation without being biased.

Anant: So, becoming a sakshi means seeing things as they really are, right?

Kapil: Yes, exactly. And when you become a sakshi, you're able to respond to life in a balanced and wise way. Imagine you're playing a video game and you're getting too involved—you might make mistakes because you're too focused on your emotions, like excitement or frustration. But if you can step back and watch carefully, without letting those emotions take over, you'll play better. Life is like that too—when we view situations with a calm and balanced mind, we make better choices.

Anant: That makes sense. But how can we apply that in our everyday lives?

Kapil: It's a practice, Anant. Start by being aware of your emotions and how they influence your actions. When you feel yourself getting too attached to an outcome or a person, pause and take a deep breath. Remind yourself to step back and observe. Over time, it becomes easier to keep a witness attitude in all situations.

MCQ

What is the meaning of "Sakshi Bhava"?

a) Becoming overly attached to outcomes.

b) The attitude of a witness, observing without judgment.

c) Strong emotional involvement in situations.

d) Ignoring people's mistakes.

What do attachments do to our judgment, according to Kapil?

a) They make us see the whole truth clearly.

b) They help us love everyone equally.

c) They cloud our judgment and cause bias.

d) They make it easier to understand others.

What does it mean to "offer your actions to the Divine"?

a) Only do spiritual rituals.

b) Approach every action with devotion and purpose.

c) Expect rewards for your good deeds.

d) Stop doing everyday tasks.

Answers: B, C, B

Anant: What about how we live our daily lives? Should we apply this to everything we do?

Kapil: Yes, in fact, Krishna says that whatever we do—whether it's eating, working, exercising, or even giving something to others—should be done as an offering to the Divine. If we do everything with the attitude of giving it up to something higher, we begin to see life itself as a spiritual practice. Every action becomes a way to connect with the Divine. When you do your best in everything, and offer that effort up, you are living a life of karma yoga, the yoga of selfless action.

Anant: So, it's not just about rituals and prayers—everything can be part of our spiritual practice?

Kapil: Exactly! When you approach everything with the mindset of offering it to something greater, you live with a sense of purpose and devotion. Even small acts like helping a friend or doing chores can become ways to express your devotion. And when we live this way, we also learn to look at others with more compassion. Instead of judging them for their mistakes, we feel understanding.

Anant: But what if someone makes a lot of mistakes? Shouldn't we call them out?

Kapil: We can guide others when necessary, but always with kindness and understanding.

When someone makes a mistake, we shouldn't condemn them. We should remember that everyone has the potential to change. Behind every saint, there was once a sinner, and in front of every sinner, there is a potential saint. Nothing in life is fixed. Just because someone has made mistakes doesn't mean they're doomed forever. Everyone can grow.

Anant: That's a really hopeful way of seeing things. So, instead of being harsh, we should help people grow?

Kapil: Yes, exactly. Real bhakti, or devotion, comes with tremendous compassion. A person with a true devotional heart understands that everyone is on a journey, and sometimes we stumble along the way. Instead of being harsh and critical, we should offer support and understanding. And remember, people can change. If we can see the potential for goodness in others, we can inspire them to become better.

Anant: That's a really good way to live. It reminds me of how I want people to see me—understanding and not harsh.

Kapil: Exactly. Just like you want others to be kind and patient with you, you should be the same with others. Life is constantly changing, and so are people. If we view the world with compassion and a sakshi bhava, we'll be able to help others while growing spiritually ourselves.

Anant: I'm really starting to see how important it is to look beyond appearances and be patient with everyone's journey. I want to practice that more.

Kapil: That's a wonderful goal, Anant. When you practice seeing the best in others and offer your actions as a form of devotion, you'll find that life itself becomes a sacred and fulfilling journey.

Anant: I guess I have a lot to practice, but I'm excited to start seeing the world with more compassion and understanding.

Did You Know?

Research indicates that people can form first impressions in just milliseconds. A study published in Psychological Science found that judgments about someone's trustworthiness can be made in as little as 100 milliseconds.

Mantra:

Ekam Sat Vipra Bahudha Vadanti
This verse comes from the Rigveda and teaches that there is only one ultimate reality or truth, but people interpret and understand it in different ways. Just like different rivers all flow into the same ocean, various religions, philosophies, and beliefs are all paths that lead to the same Divine truth. It reminds us to respect different perspectives and understand that, even though we may call the Divine by different names, we are all talking about the same higher reality.

Gyan

Why should we look beyond appearances when judging someone?
a) Appearances are always accurate.
b) What's inside is more important than how someone looks.
c) Outer appearances reflect inner qualities.
d) People with simple appearances are always wrong.

Answers: B

Karm: Design a Flower of Values

Draw a flower and write values or qualities you admire in its petals. Choose any flower you like, and fill the petals with words that represent the inner qualities you want to cultivate, like kindness, honesty, or courage.

Chapter 21: The Balance of Good and Bad

Anant: Kapil, sometimes I feel like things are either really good or really bad. I mean, how do we know what's really "good" and what's "bad"? Can something come from the same source but still be both?

Kapil: That's a very thoughtful question, Anant. The truth is, what we see as "good" and "bad" are just two sides of the same coin. Everything, even things we think are bad, comes from the same source—just like how day and night both come from the same sky. Let me explain it through some qualities that come from the Divine.

Anant: Like what qualities?

Kapil: Qualities like wisdom and intelligence—these are called buddhih and jnana. When we act with clarity and understanding, we're showing these qualities. Then there's asammudhah, which means being free from confusion, able to see things clearly, and ksama, which is the ability to forgive others and let go of anger.

Anant: That sounds like a lot of qualities!

Kapil: There are more! For example, satyam, which means truthfulness, and damah and samah, which are self-control and calmness. These are important when we want to stay balanced, especially when things don't go our way.

And then there's sukham and dukham—happiness and sadness. Both of these are part of life.

Anant: But if happiness comes from the Divine, why does sadness too?

Kapil: Good question! It's because sukham and dukham, like all emotions, are part of the human experience. Both come from the same source, and we need both to learn and grow. Imagine a plant—it needs sunlight, but it also needs rain. If it had only sunshine, it wouldn't grow properly.

Anant: So, what about other emotions like fear?

Kapil: Bhayam (fear) and abhayam (fearlessness) are also part of life. Fear can protect us, like when we avoid dangerous situations, but too much fear can hold us back. The key is to understand both, without letting them control us.

There's also ahimsa, which means non-violence, and samata, which means treating everyone equally. Being kind and peaceful helps us stay balanced. And then we have tustih, which is contentment—being satisfied with what we have, instead of always wanting more.

Anant: What if we want more sometimes? Is that bad?

Kapil: Not necessarily! Wanting more is natural, but we must balance it with tapas —self-discipline. This helps us focus on what really matters. There's also danam, or generosity, which teaches us to share with others, and yasah and ayasah, which represent fame and disgrace. Both of these can come and go, and neither should control our happiness.

Anant: Wow, there's so much to learn! But how does all of this help us figure out what's good or bad?

Kapil: Let me give you an example. Take carbon dioxide. For us, breathing in too much of it is bad, but for plants, it's what they need to live and grow. Or think about fire—it can cook our food, which is good, but it can also burn things, which is harmful. The same thing can be good in one situation and bad in another.

Anant: So, even things that seem bad can have a purpose?

Kapil: Exactly! Good and bad are relative. The same force creates both, and both can teach us something. When we learn to accept this, we develop what's called sakshi bhava—the witness attitude. It helps us see things as they are, without getting caught up in whether they're good or bad. Imagine you're standing on a hill, watching cars pass by on a road below. You can see them coming and going, but you're not driving any of the cars—you're just observing. That's what sakshi bhava feels like in life. You're aware of everything happening, but you're not pulled into the emotions or judgments attached to those events.

Did You Know?

Some of the most dangerous toxins, like snake venom, are used to create life-saving medications. For example, certain venom components are studied to treat heart conditions. This shows that what seems harmful can have positive uses.

MCQ

What qualities are associated with clarity and understanding?
a) Satyam and sukham
b) Ksama and dukham
c) Buddhih and jnana
d) Tapas and samata

Which two qualities represent happiness and sadness?
a) Sukham and dukham
b) Bhayam and abhayam
c) Damah and samah
d) Tustih and tapas

Answers: C, A

Anant: So, the key is to understand both sides and not get carried away by one or the other?

Kapil: You've got it! When you understand the balance of life, you grow in wisdom. By learning to see beyond "good" and "bad," you'll find peace no matter what happens. Instead of reacting quickly—like getting overly excited when something good happens, or feeling defeated when things go wrong—you stay calm and steady. This doesn't mean ignoring your emotions, but rather, being able to step back and say, "Okay, this is happening, and I'm just going to observe it without letting it control me."

Anant: That makes sense. I guess everything really is connected in a way, even the things we don't always like.

Kapil: Exactly, Anant. Everything comes from the same source, and when we realize that, we find harmony in life. Sakshi bhava allows us to appreciate that connection and see the lessons in all experiences. Whether we view something as "good" or "bad," the key is to watch it with awareness, knowing that it all plays a role in our growth.

Let me give you an example. Imagine you're playing in a soccer game, and your team is losing. You start to feel angry or disappointed, and you might even blame yourself or your teammates. But if you adopt sakshi bhava, you step back and observe the situation without judgment. You notice your emotions, but you don't let them take control. Instead, you see the game as just one moment, one experience, and understand that whether you win or lose, it's part of the bigger picture. You still try your best, but you don't get carried away by the outcome.

Anant: Wow, that sounds really hard to do, but I can see how it would make things easier to handle.

Kapil: It can be challenging, but with practice, you can develop sakshi bhava. Over time, it helps you handle situations with more calmness and clarity, without being overwhelmed by the ups and downs.

Anant: I think if I can practice seeing things like that, life will feel a lot lighter, even when things don't go my way.

Mantra:

Maya Tatam Idam Sarvam

Meaning:Imagine the air around us. We can't always see it, but it's everywhere —inside, outside, in every corner. Similarly, the Divine is like that air, present in everything we see and feel, even if we don't always notice it.

Gyan:

What does tapas represent?
a) Generosity
b) Self-discipline
c) Fame
d) Contentment

Which of the following qualities helps us treat everyone equally?
a) Samata
b) Tustih
c) Damah
d) Ksama

Answers: B, A

Karm: Ksama

Write a letter to someone you've been upset with. In this letter, explain how you feel, why the situation bothered you, and offer your forgiveness, even if you choose not to send the letter. After writing, take a moment to reflect on how it feels to let go of the anger or hurt. Does it bring relief? Does it change how you view the situation or the person? Use this as an opportunity to explore the power of forgiveness.

Chapter 22: Understanding Dharma and Respecting All Paths

Anant: Kapil, I've been thinking about how things are always changing. Does that mean the way we live and the rules we follow should change too?

Kapil: That's a great observation, Anant. In fact, there are two kinds of dharma, or principles of living. One is called Sanatana Dharma and the other is Yuga Dharma. Sanatana Dharma is the eternal and universal truth. It never changes. It includes values like truth, compassion, and non-violence—things that are always good for everyone, no matter the time or place.

Anant: So, Sanatana Dharma is like the foundation we can always rely on?

Kapil: Exactly. But there is also Yuga Dharma, which is the set of rules and practices that change based on the time, place, and the specific needs of a society. Every age, or yuga, has its own challenges and situations. Yuga Dharma adapts to meet those challenges. What might be right or necessary in one age could be completely different in another. So, while Sanatana Dharma stays the same, Yuga Dharma changes as needed.

Anant: That makes sense. So, Sanatana Dharma is like a constant, and Yuga Dharma is more flexible?

Kapil: Yes, that's a good way to put it. Think about it this way: in the past, people lived in a very different world with different kinds of challenges, so their Yuga Dharma was based on what was needed then. Now, we live in a world with modern technology and new challenges, so our Yuga Dharma looks different. But the core values of Sanatana Dharma, like kindness and honesty, remain unchanged.

Anant: I get it now. But Kapil, there's a verse I remember where Krishna says, "Whenever there is a decline of dharma and a rise of adharma, I come forth." What does that mean?

Kapil: Ah, yes. That's one of the most important teachings in the Gita. Krishna is saying that whenever goodness, or dharma, starts to fade and badness, or adharma, begins to grow, he will come to restore balance. He might come as a person, a teacher, a guide, or even as an idea or inspiration in someone's heart. The point is, Krishna is always present, ready to help set things right when the world needs it most.

Anant: So, Krishna helps whenever things go wrong?

Kapil: Yes, but there's more to it than that. Krishna also teaches us that we should do our part to keep dharma alive. We can't just wait for help from above. We have to live by dharma—by doing what's right—even when it's hard. Krishna is there to guide us, but we also have a responsibility to live in a way that keeps goodness and balance in the world

Did You Know?

Krishna, often depicted playing a flute, symbolizes harmony and balance, representing how spiritual wisdom can create a melodious life.

Anant: I see. So, it's not just about waiting for divine help, but also about taking action ourselves?

Kapil: Exactly. Dharma is about living in harmony with the world and the people around us. And that means we have to do our part to create and maintain that harmony. Sometimes, it's small actions, like being kind to others, and sometimes it's bigger, like standing up for what's right.
Anant: Kapil, Krishna also says that all paths lead to him and that we shouldn't fight in the name of religion. Can you explain that?

Kapil: Yes, Anant. This is another important teaching from Krishna. What he's saying is that no matter what path someone follows—whether it's through prayer, meditation, helping others, or worship—it will lead to him, as long as it's done with sincerity and goodness. People may have different religions, beliefs, or ways of worship, but the goal is the same: to find and connect with the divine

Anant: So, it doesn't matter which path we choose, as long as we're sincere?

MCQ

What are the two types of dharma mentioned in the lesson?

a) Karma and Bhakti

b) Sanatana Dharma and Yuga Dharma

c) Krishna Dharma and Ram Dharma

d) Moksha Dharma and Yuga Dharma

Answer: b) Sanatana Dharma and Yuga Dharma

Which dharma is considered eternal and unchanging?

a) Sanatana Dharma

b) Yuga Dharma

c) Karma Dharma

d) Bhakti Dharma

Answer: b) Sanatana Dharma

Yuga Dharma refers to:

a) Timeless and universal values

b) Values that change based on time and society's needs

c) Teachings of Krishna

d) The concept of reincarnation

Answers: B, A, B

Kapil: Exactly. We should respect all paths and never argue or fight about whose way is better. What matters is that we live with love, respect, and understanding. Krishna teaches us to see the good in all paths and focus on what brings us closer to him and to each other.

Anant: That's a really beautiful way to look at it. It means we don't have to fight over who's right, as long as we're all trying to do good.

Kapil: You're absolutely right, Anant. The idea is to live with openness and compassion, recognizing that everyone's journey is different but ultimately leading to the same truth. When we respect and honor each other's paths, we create a world where everyone can grow spiritually and live in peace.

Anant: It seems like everything Krishna teaches is about finding balance and harmony, whether it's with ourselves, others, or the world around us.

Kapil: Yes, Anant, that's exactly it. Krishna's teachings remind us that life is about balance—balancing action and reflection, self-interest and selflessness, and respecting the many ways people seek the truth. If we live in balance, we live in harmony with the divine. But to explain further, this balance is not just about how we act but also about how we think and perceive the world.

For example, balance in action means knowing when to push forward and when to step back and reflect.

Sometimes we're so caught up in chasing our goals that we forget to pause and think about the bigger picture. Krishna teaches us that while action is important, it should always be guided by reflection and wisdom. Acting without thinking can lead us astray, but thinking without acting can make us stagnant. Balance means finding the middle ground.

Then, there's balance between self-interest and selflessness. It's natural to want things for ourselves, but if we live only for our desires, we'll feel disconnected from others. On the other hand, if we only focus on others and neglect ourselves, we can burn out. Krishna teaches us that it's okay to seek personal happiness, but we should also be mindful of how our actions affect those around us. True harmony comes from serving both ourselves and others.

Finally, there's balance in how we view the paths of others. People have different beliefs, different ways of worship, and different journeys in life. Respecting these differences instead of judging them is key to living in harmony. If we constantly argue about whose way is better, we create conflict. But if we see that all sincere paths lead to the same truth, we can live with more understanding and peace.

Anant: I'll remember that. Balance and harmony—it seems like the key to everything.

Mantra:

Tasmat Tvam Uttistha

The mantra "Tasmat Tvam Uttistha" comes from the Bhagavad Gita, and it translates to "Therefore, stand up!" or "Therefore, arise!" In this context, Krishna is urging Arjuna to rise and fulfill his duty.

Gyan:

What is the role of individuals in maintaining dharma according to Krishna?

a) Waiting for divine intervention

b) Taking action to keep goodness and balance in the world

c) Focusing on personal gain

d) Praying for guidance only in tough times

Why does Krishna say we should not fight over religious beliefs?

a) Because no religion is more important than others

b) Because it is written in Yuga Dharma to avoid arguments

c) Because fighting is part of Yuga Dharma

d) Because all paths, when followed with sincerity, lead to the same truth

Answers: B, D

Karm: Yuga

Color the Sun (Sanatana Dharma - eternal truth) and the Clock (Yuga Dharma - changing with time). As you color the sun, think about unchanging values like truth and kindness. While coloring the clock, reflect on how rules and customs adapt with time.

This activity helps you understand the difference between Sanatana Dharma (eternal truth) and Yuga Dharma (changing principles). Enjoy coloring and reflect on how both guide us!

Chapter 23: The Qualities of a True Devotee

Anant: Kapil, I've been thinking about the different paths in yoga you've told me about, like Bhakti and Jnana. Which one is better? Is one easier than the other?

Kapil: That's a really good question, Anant. Both paths—Bhakti and Jnana—are valid and lead us to the divine, but they're different in how we approach them. Jnana Yoga, the path of knowledge, is often more difficult. It's about understanding Brahman, which is infinite and beyond our normal thinking. We have to detach ourselves from everything worldly—our desires, our attachments. It's tough because it requires a lot of inner work and deep self-discipline.

Anant: So, is Bhakti easier?

Kapil: Yes, for most people, Bhakti Yoga is easier. Bhakti is the path of devotion, where instead of detaching from everything, you simply offer your love and devotion to the divine. There's no need to wipe away all your attachments right away. You can still live in the world and find your connection to the divine through love and devotion. That makes Bhakti a more accessible path for many.

Anant: I see. So, Bhakti is more practical for most people. But what if someone can't focus their mind on the divine all the time? What can they do?

Kapil: That's a great point, Anant. If it's hard to keep your mind focused on the divine, then you can practice Abhyasa Yoga. Abhyasa means continual effort. It's like practicing any skill—whether it's learning to play an instrument or getting better at a sport. Over time, with steady effort, you improve. The same goes for spiritual practice. If you make the effort, even if it's difficult at first, it will get easier.

Anant: So, it's like building a habit?

Kapil: Exactly. Just like how you become better at something with repetition, continual effort in yoga helps you strengthen your focus on the divine. But if even that seems too hard, there's another step. You can perform all your actions as a dedication to the divine. That means everything you do, whether it's work, study, or even helping someone, you do it as an offering to the divine. When you dedicate your actions, your whole life becomes a form of worship.

Anant: I like that. It seems easier to start by offering actions rather than trying to keep the mind focused all the time.

Kapil: It is. And Krishna teaches us that this gradual approach is just as valid. Now, let's talk about the qualities of a true devotee, someone who has followed the path of Bhakti and dedicated their life to the divine.

Anant: What are those qualities?Could you list and explain them more clearly? I think it would help me understand better.

Kapil: Sure, Anant. Here's a list of the qualities of a true devotee, and I'll explain each one in detail.

- No enmity towards any being: A true devotee doesn't harbor any hatred or ill will towards anyone. They see the divine in all beings and approach life with love and compassion.
- Friend to all: They are naturally friendly and kind to everyone. Their heart is open, and they offer love and understanding to others without expecting anything in return.
- Free from the idea of "it is mine": A devotee does not cling to possessiveness. They understand that nothing truly belongs to them, and they remain detached from material things and outcomes.
- Gentle ego: Instead of having an inflated ego, they carry what we call a "gentle ego"—an ego of humility and devotion. They don't act out of pride or self-importance but out of love for the divine.
- Even-minded in pain and pleasure: A true devotee remains calm and composed in both good and bad times. They don't get too elated when things go well or too distressed when they don't.
- Forgiving: They are quick to forgive others and let go of grudges. Forgiveness is a key trait, as they understand that holding onto negativity only causes more harm.

MCQ

What is the key characteristic of Bhakti Yoga?

a) Detachment from the world

b) Focus on devotion to the divine

c) Acquiring spiritual knowledge

d) Controlling the senses

A true devotee is said to be:

a) Agitated by the world but hides it

b) Completely detached from society

c) Unshaken by the world and causes no disturbance to others

d) Overjoyed by material successes

Which of the following is NOT a quality of a true devotee?

a) Possessiveness over material things

b) Steadiness in meditation

c) Forgiveness

d) Purity of heart

Answers: B, C, A

- Ever content: A devotee is satisfied with whatever comes their way. Whether they have much or little, they find peace in every situation because they trust in the divine plan.
- Steady in meditation: They maintain a regular practice of meditation, keeping their mind focused on the divine. This consistency helps them stay grounded and spiritually aligned.
- Self-controlled: A devotee has mastery over their senses and desires. They don't let impulses or emotions take over but remain disciplined in their actions and thoughts.
- Not agitated by the world: A true devotee is unshaken by the chaos and distractions of the outside world. They remain peaceful and calm, no matter what's happening around them.
- Cannot be agitated by the world: Just as they are not disturbed by the world, they also don't cause disturbance to others. They live in a way that brings peace to themselves and those around them.
- Free from excessive joy, intolerance, fear, and anxiety: They don't swing between extremes of emotion. They don't experience overwhelming joy or despair, and they are free from fears and worries.
- Free from dependence: A devotee is independent of external circumstances for their happiness. They are self-sufficient because their contentment comes from within, from their connection to the divine.
- Pure in heart: Their intentions are always pure. They act out of goodness, with no hidden motives or selfish desires.
- Prompt: They are always ready to act when needed. A true devotee is never lazy or procrastinating, but always alert and proactive in their duties.

- Unconcerned with worldly troubles: While they live in the world, they don't get caught up in the temporary ups and downs of life. Their focus remains on the higher purpose.
- Firm conviction: They have strong faith in their path and the divine. No matter what challenges arise, they hold firm to their beliefs and stay devoted.
- Neither rejoices nor hates, nor grieves nor desires: They remain neutral and balanced. They don't get too attached to happiness, nor do they grieve over losses. They live with a sense of detachment and inner peace.
- Same to friend and foe: They treat everyone equally, whether it's someone who is kind to them or someone who opposes them. They see all beings as part of the divine.
- Same in honor and dishonor: A true devotee doesn't seek praise, nor do they get upset when criticized. They remain steady, unaffected by what others think of them.
- Same in heat and cold, pleasure and pain: Whether it's physical discomfort or emotional ups and downs, a devotee maintains the same calmness. They are unaffected by external conditions.
- Same in censure and praise: They treat both criticism and compliments with equal calmness. They don't let praise boost their ego, nor do they let criticism bring them down.
- Silent and content with anything: A true devotee speaks only when necessary and is content with whatever life offers. They don't demand more but remain satisfied with what they have.

Anant: Wow, Kapil, that's a lot to live up to! But I can see how these qualities would bring a lot of peace and balance to someone's life. It's like becoming the best version of yourself.

Kapil: Yes, Anant. But remember, it's a journey. By following the path of Bhakti or practicing Abhyasa Yoga, and dedicating your actions, you can cultivate those qualities over time. What matters most is sincerity and effort.

Anant: I understand now. Whether it's through Bhakti or Jnana, it's all about steady progress and dedication.

Did You Know?

Research shows that forgiving others reduces cortisol levels (the stress hormone), lowers blood pressure, and improves heart health. It's like a natural stress reliever!

Mantra:

Na Tvat Samo Asti

Meaning: There is none equal to You.

This shloka is used in praise of a divine being, acknowledging that no one and nothing can compare to the supreme power and greatness of the divine. It expresses reverence, showing that the qualities, strength, and wisdom of the divine are unparalleled and unmatched. In essence, it says that the divine is unique and beyond comparison.

Gyan:

What does "free from dependence" mean for a true devotee?

a) They rely on external circumstances for happiness

b) They are dependent on others for their spiritual progress

c) They find happiness and peace from within, not from outside

d) They are dependent on material success

Answers: C

Karm: Create Your Own Devotee Shield:

Using the blank shield template, design a shield with symbols or words that represent the qualities of a true devotee, such as peace, kindness, and forgiveness. Think about how each quality can protect and guide you in life. Draw or write symbols that express these values—like a heart for love or a dove for peace—and add colors to reflect how they make you feel.

Chapter 24: The Body and Spiritual Knowledge

Anant: Kapil, last time we talked about different paths like Bhakti and Jnana. But what about our bodies? How do they fit into all of this?

Kapil: That's a great question, Anant. Our body is called kshetra, which means the "field." Think of it like a piece of land. The one who knows the body and what it's capable of is called ksetrajna—the "knower of the field."

Anant: So, kshetra is like the physical body, and ksetrajna is the one who understands it?

Kapil: Exactly! And there are two parts to this. First, we have the physical aspect—the body made up of earth, water, fire, space, air, and ego. This is the part of us that changes, gets hungry, tired, grows, and eventually gets old.

Anant: That's the part we can see, right?

Kapil: Yes, that's right. But then there's the spiritual aspect. This is our higher nature, the pure intelligence that stays the same. It's like the center of the universe that never changes. The physical part, or kshetra, comes and goes, but the spiritual part is beyond that.

Anant: I see. So, the body changes, but the spiritual part stays the same?

Kapil: Exactly! The physical part is like the world around us, constantly changing. But at the center of it all is pure intelligence, which is unchanging. Understanding this difference is really important in our spiritual journey.

Anant: How do we gain true spiritual knowledge then? Is it by understanding this difference?

Kapil: Yes, but true spiritual knowledge also comes from developing certain moral qualities and virtues. These qualities help us to see beyond just the physical and connect with our higher nature.

Anant: What kind of qualities are we talking about?

Kapil: Well, to start, humility—being modest and not thinking too highly of ourselves. Then, unpretentiousness, which means not pretending to be something we're not. Non-injury is another key one—it means we should try not to harm others in thought, word, or action.

Anant: That sounds hard! What else?

Kapil: Forbearance, or patience, is important. Uprightness means being honest and truthful. Then there's service to the teacher, which helps us stay humble and learn from others. Purity and steadiness are also necessary for spiritual growth.

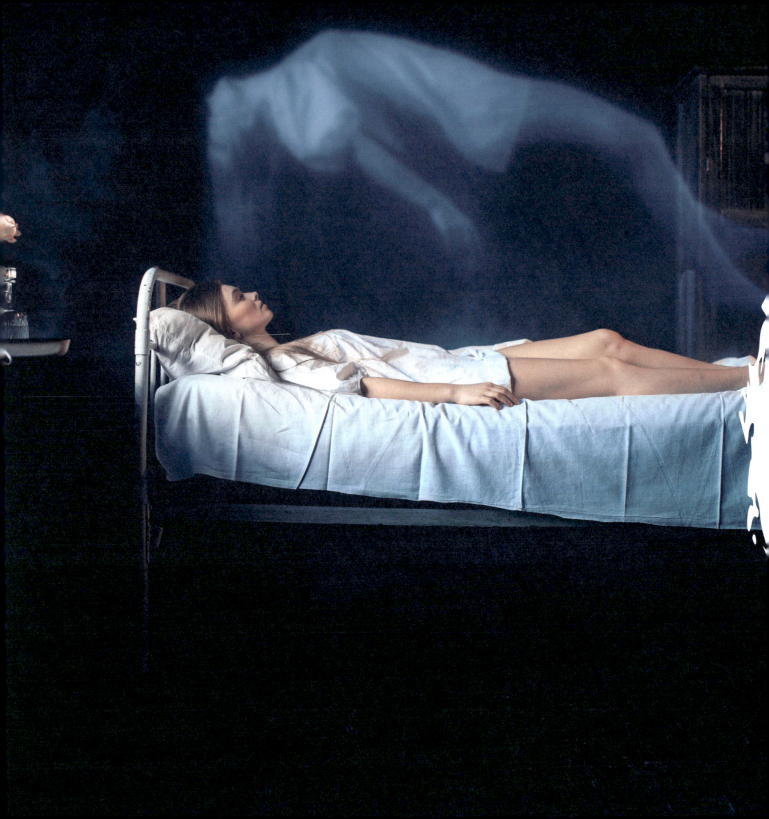

MCQ

What is the term used for the physical body in spiritual knowledge?

a) Ksetrajna

b) Kshetra

c) Atman

d) Prakriti

Which of the following is considered the unchanging part of us?

a) Body

b) Mind

c) Pure Intelligence

d) Ego

Answers: B, C

Did you know:

Seeing the Atman in All: In evolutionary biology, the recognition of shared human experiences fosters cooperation and community. This concept mirrors empathy, where understanding the oneness of life encourages kindness and prevents harm to others.

Anant: And what about things like self-control?

Kapil: Yes, self-control is essential. It means we control our desires instead of letting them control us. It's also important to renounce excessive attachment to sense objects—meaning we shouldn't get too caught up in chasing things like food, entertainment, or possessions.

Anant: So, don't be too attached to things?

Kapil: Exactly! There should also be an absence of egoism, where we don't always think about "me" and "mine."

Anant: That's a lot to remember! Is there anything else?

Kapil: Yes, non-attachment, which means not holding on to things too tightly. Non-identification of the self with others means we shouldn't compare ourselves with others all the time. Being even-minded in both good and bad times is also very important.

Anant: So, it's about staying calm no matter what happens?

Kapil: Yes, and the last few qualities are really important too. Tremendous devotion to the divine helps us stay connected to something higher. Spending some time alone in silence is also necessary because it helps us reflect. Finally, the constant pursuit of spiritual knowledge will guide us on this journey.

Anant: Wow! That's a lot of qualities to work on. But I guess they all help us to see things clearly and find peace.

Kapil: Exactly, Anant. These qualities help us move beyond just the physical body and truly understand the spiritual part of ourselves. It's like clearing a path that leads us to true knowledge.

Kapil: It is, but all of these qualities help us grow spiritually. We also need to reflect on the challenges of life like birth, death, old age, sickness, and pain, and understand that everything in the world is temporary.

Anant: And when we practice all these things, we see the world differently?

Kapil: Absolutely. You start to realize that the same atman, or soul, is present in everyone, no matter if they're rich or poor, educated or uneducated. When you see the atman in others, you don't harm them. And when you understand the atman within yourself, you don't harm yourself either.

Anant: So even if our senses, mind, or intellect can be influenced by bad things, the atman always stays pure?

Kapil: Exactly! The atman is beyond all of that. It can't be touched by evil or sin. It's like the sun, always shining behind the clouds. No matter what happens to our bodies or minds, the atman remains perfect and unchanging. When you see that in others and yourself, you live in harmony with the world.

Mantra:

Bhajan: Ramratan Maine Payo

Meaning: I have received the Ramratan, the Gem of Rama in my heart

Gyan:

Which of the following elements are part of the physical body, according to Kapil?

a) Ego and Intelligence

b) Earth, water, fire, space, and air

c) Emotions and desires

d) Karma and Dharma

What helps us reflect on the challenges of life like birth, death, and old age?

a) Silence and solitude

b) Attachment to sense objects

c) Egoism

d) Non-identification of the self

Answers: B, A

Karm: Body as the Field (Kshetra) Drawing

Draw an outline of your body and label it "Kshetra." Inside the outline, write things related to your body, like feeling hungry, tired, or growing. Outside the body, write down what helps you understand these feelings—like being aware of them or noticing how you feel.

Chapter 25: Discovering Our True Nature

Anant: Kapil, I've been thinking. Why do human beings forget their true nature? We're supposed to be connected to something greater, but it's like we get distracted.

Kapil: That's a great question, Anant. Human beings forget their essential nature due to the influence of prakrti, or nature. This nature has three fundamental qualities or gunas: Sattva, Rajas, and Tamas. These three forces are constantly acting upon us, shaping how we feel, think, and act.

Anant: I've heard of them, but how exactly do they work?

Kapil: Let's start with Sattva. Sattva is pure, transparent, luminous, and stainless. Wherever there is serenity, happiness, joy, or knowledge, Sattva is at work. It's the force that makes us feel calm and peaceful, like when we're in nature or when we're deeply content. However, even though Sattva brings clarity, it also binds us—because we can become attached to the happiness and knowledge it brings.

Anant: So, we get attached to feeling good or being wise?

Kapil: Exactly. That's how *Sattva* binds us. It's subtle, but it still creates attachment. Now, *Rajas* is different. *Rajas* is the force of passion and action.

Wherever there's craving, excitement, or a strong desire to accomplish something, Rajas is dominating. But the downside is that Rajas binds us through attachment to action. We become restless, constantly planning and doing, always wanting more.

Anant: That sounds exhausting.

Kapil: It is. Rajas creates a sense of never being satisfied. You always want to do more, achieve more, and it can lead to sorrow when those desires aren't fulfilled. Then, there's Tamas. Tamas is the quality of ignorance. When Tamas dominates, there's delusion, confusion, and a lack of awareness. It's what makes us feel lazy, tired, and uninterested in life. It clouds our minds, and everything feels heavy and dull.

Anant: So Tamas is like when we feel really low and can't be bothered to do anything?

Kapil: Exactly. Tamas creates inertia. You feel sleepy, unmotivated, and just don't want to act. It makes everything seem unclear, and it's the hardest to overcome because it keeps us in a state of ignorance.

Anant: But can we shift between these three forces?

Kapil: Absolutely. These *gunas* are constantly shifting within us. When *Sattva* dominates, we feel light, joyful, and serene.

MCQ

What are the three gunas that influence human behavior?

a) Sattva, Karma, and Bhakti

b) Sattva, Rajas, and Tamas

c) Dharma, Artha, and Moksha

d) Sattva, Tamas, and Prakriti

2. What is the quality of Sattva?

a) It brings restlessness and desire

b) It creates delusion and laziness

c) It brings serenity, joy, and knowledge

d) It makes everything seem heavy and unclear

Answers: B, C

All our senses are calm, and we're able to gain wisdom and see things clearly. When Rajas dominates, we become restless, active, and full of desire. And when Tamas takes over, we fall into darkness and laziness, losing all sense of direction.

Anant: Is there a way to know when one of them is taking over?

Kapil: Yes. When you experience lightness, serenity, and clarity, you can be sure that Sattva is in charge. But when you feel restless, greedy, or always thinking of the next action, Rajas is predominant. And if you feel sleepy, confused, or have no desire to do anything, then Tamas is taking over.

Anant: What happens as a result of these forces?

Kapil: The results of actions depend on which guna is in charge. When Sattva guides your actions, the outcome is pure and positive. But actions driven by Rajas lead to more suffering because they're based on desire and attachment. And actions dominated by Tamas result in ignorance and confusion.

Anant: So, to be truly happy and peaceful, we should aim to strengthen Sattva?

Kapil: Exactly. By cultivating *Sattva* through knowledge, discipline, and detachment, you can bring more light into your life. But it's important to understand that these *gunas* are always present and always shifting.

The key is to observe them and not let them control you. The more you understand their influence, the more freedom you'll find.

Anant: So, the goal is not to get rid of the gunas but to learn how to manage them?

Kapil: Yes, but even beyond managing them, the ultimate goal is to transcend the gunas. The human being who is beyond the three gunas—Sattva, Rajas, and Tamas—does not become unhappy when they are active. They also don't feel longing for them if they do not manifest.

Anant: Wait, what does that mean? If the gunas are always there, how can someone just not be affected by them?

Kapil: It's about developing complete indifference to the coming and going of the gunas and their effects. When you reach this state, whether Sattva brings you joy or Tamas pulls you into lethargy, you remain unmoved. You understand that these are just temporary fluctuations of nature, not who you truly are.

Anant: So, it's like watching a storm pass by without getting caught in it?

Kapil: Exactly! You become the observer, knowing that the storm will come and go, but you remain steady. This is what Krishna calls being a sthitaprajna, someone who is firm in wisdom. They are completely indifferent to the effects of the gunas, neither craving their presence nor feeling sorrow when they pass.

Anant: That sounds like a really peaceful way to live. But is it really possible to get to that point?

Kapil: It is possible, Anant, but it takes practice—just like anything else. Through consistent self-awareness and meditation, you slowly train yourself to rise above the influence of the gunas. The first step is recognizing when they are at work, and then, over time, you learn not to identify with them.

Anant: So, even when I feel restless or lazy, I should just observe it and not let it define me?

Kapil: Yes. Understand that restlessness is Rajas at work, and laziness is Tamas influencing you. But beyond all these qualities, your true self—the Atman—remains untouched. By focusing on that higher self, you can remain at peace, regardless of which guna is active.

Anant: I think I understand. It's about seeing the bigger picture, right?

Kapil: Exactly. The gunas belong to the body and mind, but the soul is beyond them. When you keep that in mind, you won't be swayed by their temporary effects.

Anant: I see now—it's like being the sky, watching the clouds come and go, but knowing that the sky itself never changes.

Mantra:

Cidānandarūpah Śivoham Śivoham

Meaning: "I am made of pure awareness and happiness; I am Shiva, I am Shiva."

Gyan:

When Sattva dominates, how does one feel?

a) Restless and eager to act

b) Lazy and confused

c) Calm, joyful, and clear-headed

d) Tired and uninterested in life

What happens when Rajas dominates?

a) You feel calm and content

b) You become restless and filled with desire

c) You feel sleepy and unmotivated

d) You become more aware of your higher self

Answers: C, B

Karm: Match the Actions with the Three Gunas

Below are different actions. Draw a line to match each action with the correct guna—Sattva (Balance), Rajas (Activity), or Tamas (Inertia).

1. Helping a friend with homework

2. Arguing with a classmate

3. Skipping schoolwork to sleep

4. Meditating for calmness

5. Feeling restless and impatient

6. Avoiding responsibilities

a. Sattva (Balance)

b. Rajas (Activity)

c. Tamas (Inertia)

Chapter 26: The Tree of the Universe

Anant: Kapil, I often think about the universe. What can we liken the universe to?

Kapil: I'm glad you asked, Anant. This is an important teaching in the Gita, and it might seem a little strange at first. The universe is often described as an eternal Ashvattha or Pipal tree. This tree is unique because it's inverted—its roots are above, and its branches stretch below. Think of the roots as being connected to Brahman, the divine source of everything. The branches represent everything that exists in the world—both physical and spiritual. This cosmic tree symbolizes how life flows from the divine, spreading out and taking many forms.

Anant: So the roots represent Brahman? What about the branches?

Kapil: The branches represent everything we experience—the entire material world and even the celestial realms above. Everything that exists comes from that one root, Brahman. The branches are nourished by the three gunas, which are qualities that bind the universe together: Sattva, Rajas, and Tamas. These three forces influence everything we do and experience.

Anant: I think I understand. But why compare the universe to a tree? What's the significance of trees in Hindu spirituality?

Kapil: Trees are very special in Hindu spirituality. They symbolize life, growth, connection, and protection. A tree stands firm, its roots buried deep, while its branches provide shelter, food, and air for living beings. It gives everything without asking for anything in return. The universe is like this tree—it provides for us, it gives us life and shelter, but it also remains beyond our control. Just as birds come and go from the branches of a tree, people come and go in the world. But the tree itself—the universe—remains constant, even though the beings within it change.

Anant: So, we are like birds on this cosmic tree, living in its branches?

Kapil: Exactly. People live, grow, and then pass on, but the universe continues. It remains, like the tree's sturdy trunk, while we are like leaves and branches that grow for a time and eventually fall away. This eternal tree has branches that spread out both above and below. The lower branches represent the terrestrial world where we live, while the higher branches stretch into the celestial world. They are all connected, and they all come from Brahman, the source of everything.

Anant: That's really interesting. But you mentioned that we need to cut this tree. Why would we want to cut it down?

Kapil: That's an important part of the teaching. While the tree represents the entire universe, it also symbolizes how we get attached to the material world. This attachment is what binds us to the cycle of birth, death, and rebirth.

Did You Know?

In quantum physics, particles can become entangled, meaning the state of one particle is directly related to the state of another, no matter the distance between them. This mirrors the Gita's teaching about the interconnectedness of all beings and the idea that everything is part of a larger whole (Brahman).

MCQ

What does the Ashvattha tree represent in Hindu philosophy?
a) The temporary nature of existence
b) The structure of human consciousness
c) The eternal universe, rooted in Brahman
d) A symbol of the human mind

What is unique about the Ashvattha tree?
a) It has flowers that never fade
b) Its roots are above and its branches below
c) It changes color with the seasons
d) It grows only in the heavens

Answers: C, B

To truly understand our higher purpose, we need to break free from this attachment. This tree is so vast and deep-rooted that we can't just cut it down easily. We need a sharp weapon to do it, and that weapon is non-attachment. Detachment is the sword we must use to sever our ties to the material world.

Anant: So, detachment is like cutting away the branches that keep us tied to the world?

Kapil: Yes, that's a good way to think of it. Detachment means not being overly attached to material things, people, or outcomes. It doesn't mean you shouldn't care or love, but it means understanding that everything here is temporary. There are three phases to everything in the universe: things come into being, they stay for a while, and then they fade away. Just like the leaves of a tree, which grow, fall, and are replaced, everything in life follows this cycle. By practicing non-attachment, we realize that nothing in this world is permanent.

Anant: So, when we let go of our attachments, we can see things as they really are?

Kapil: Exactly! When you let go of attachment, you begin to see the truth. The tree of the universe is vast and complex, but nothing in it lasts forever. By detaching yourself from temporary things, you open the door to understanding Brahman, the eternal source behind everything.

The more we free ourselves from desires and attachments, the closer we come to realizing our true nature, which is connected to Brahman.

Anant: And how do we actually connect with Brahman?

Kapil: That's the heart of the journey, Anant. We connect with Brahman by removing pride, arrogance, and delusion. These qualities keep us tied to the lower branches of the tree, focused only on the material world. By conquering the evil of attachment and practicing awareness of the Atman—the true self within—you can rise above the pairs of opposites like pleasure and pain, happiness and suffering. This constant practice of awareness is how we break free from the bonds of the tree and connect with Brahman.

Anant: So it's all about staying aware of the Atman, the true self, and letting go of attachments?

Kapil: Yes. When we realize that our true self is not tied to the changing world around us, we find peace. We are no longer trapped by the ups and downs of life—pleasure and pain, success and failure. We learn to see beyond those temporary experiences. The eternal tree of the universe may remain, but we are no longer bound to its branches. We are connected to something deeper, something unchanging—Brahman.

Anant: That makes sense. It's like finding a deeper root within ourselves, beyond the branches of the tree.

Kapil: Exactly. Once we recognize this deeper connection, we live differently. We don't get caught up in the fleeting things of life. We can enjoy the beauty of the tree, but we are no longer bound to it. We understand that everything in the material world—just like the tree—comes into being, stays for a while, and then goes. The only thing that remains constant is Brahman, the source of all creation. This is the wisdom that detachment brings, and it leads us to true freedom.

Anant: I think I'm starting to get it now. It's not about ignoring the world but understanding that there's something bigger beyond it, something we can connect to.

Kapil: Exactly, Anant. When you understand that, you find peace, because you realize that while everything in the world changes, the root, Brahman, remains unchanging and eternal. That's the real lesson of the tree of the universe.

Anant: I guess now I'll think of the universe differently—like a tree with deep roots that goes far beyond what I can see.

Mantra:

Satyam Jnaanam Anantam Brahma

The mantra "Satyam Jnaanam Anantam Brahma" describes the nature of Brahman, or the ultimate reality, in three ways:

So, this mantra tells us that Brahman, or the ultimate reality, is the eternal truth, the source of all knowledge, and infinite in nature.

Gyan:

What is nourished by the three gunas—Sattva, Rajas, and Tamas—in the cosmic tree?

a) The roots
b) The leaves and branches
c) The trunk
d) The fruits of the tree

Why does the Gita suggest cutting down the cosmic tree?

a) To stop the growth of ignorance
b) To detach from the material world
c) To nourish the roots of the tree
d) To make space for new branches

Answers: B, B

Karm: The Detachment Challenge

Challenge yourself to give up something you're attached to for one day. It could be screen time, your favorite snack, or a toy. At the end of the day, write in your journal or discuss with your group:

How did it feel to let go?

Was it hard or easy?

What did you learn from this experience?

Chapter 27: The Divine and the Demonic

Anant: Kapil, last time you talked about how we can connect to Brahman by getting rid of pride, arrogance, and attachment. But how do we know if we're on the right path or falling off it?

Kapil: That's a good question, Anant! There are two paths that people can follow, known as daivi sampat and asuri sampat. These are two sets of qualities or tendencies—one divine, and the other, demonic.

Anant: What's the difference between them?

Kapil: Daivi sampat means the qualities of the divine nature, and asuri sampat refers to the qualities of the demonic nature. Let's start with daivi sampat. These are the good qualities that help us grow spiritually and live a life connected to the divine.

Here are the qualities of daivi sampat:

- **Fearlessness**: Having courage, not being afraid to stand for what is right, and facing challenges with faith.
- **Purity of Mind:** Keeping thoughts clean and free from harmful desires.
- **Steadfastness in Knowledge and Yoga**: Staying committed to learning and practicing spiritual disciplines, like meditation or yoga.

- **Almsgiving**: Being generous and helping others by giving away things or time to those in need.
- **Control of the Senses**: Not letting the senses, like taste or touch, control your actions.
- **Devotional Acts to the Divine**: Regularly engaging in prayer, chanting, or other acts of devotion.
- **Self-Study**: Spending time learning and reflecting on spiritual texts and teachings to gather knowledge.
- **Self-Discipline**: Being able to control your thoughts and actions, especially in difficult situations.
- **Non-Injury (Ahimsa)**: Not harming any living beings, whether by action, word, or thought.
- **Truth**: Always speaking and acting in ways that are truthful and honest.
- **Absence of Anger**: Keeping calm and not letting anger rule over your mind.
- **Renunciation**: Letting go of attachments to worldly things or desires.
- **Tranquility**: Being peaceful and calm in all situations.
- **Absence of Calumny**: Not speaking badly or gossiping about others.
- **Compassion to Beings**: Showing kindness and understanding to all living creatures.
- **Non-Covetousness**: Not being greedy or wanting things that belong to others.
- **Gentleness**: Being kind and considerate in your actions and speech.
- **Modesty**: Not bragging or showing off.
- **Absence of Fickleness**: Staying consistent and not changing your mind too often without reason.

- **Energy**: Having the enthusiasm and determination to work hard.
- **Forbearance**: Being patient and enduring difficulties without getting upset.
- **Fortitude**: Staying strong and resilient in tough situations.
- **Purity**: Keeping yourself clean—both physically and mentally.
- **Absence of Hatred**: Not hating anyone, no matter what happens.
- **Absence of Pride**: Being humble and not thinking of yourself as better than others.

Anant: Wow! That's a long list of qualities to develop. It sounds hard to always be like that.

Kapil: It can be challenging, but these qualities help us become better people and stay connected to the divine. Now, let's look at the **qualities of *asuri sampat*,** which are the opposite and lead us away from the right path.

Qualities of *asuri sampat*:
- Ostentation: Showing off and wanting to appear better than others.
- Arrogance: Having too much pride and thinking you are more important than everyone else.
- Self-Conceit: Being overly proud of yourself and thinking too highly of your own abilities.
- Anger: Letting anger control you and reacting harshly.
- Harshness: Being rude and not caring about other people's feelings.
- Ignorance: Not knowing the truth and not even trying to understand it.
- Lack of Purity: Not caring about keeping your mind or body clean.

Did you know?

In chaos theory, the butterfly effect suggests that small actions can lead to significant changes. This connects with the idea that each good or bad quality influences our life trajectory and impacts others, much like how small, positive actions can lead to greater peace and happiness.

MCQ

What are the two paths people can follow according to Kapil?
a) Sattva and Tamas
b) Daivi sampat and Asuri sampat
c) Rajas and Tamas
d) Moksha and Karma

Which of the following is a quality of Daivi sampat?
a) Arrogance
b) Fearlessness
c) Ignorance
d) Insatiable Desires

Answers: B, B

- Bad Conduct: Acting in ways that are harmful or dishonest.
- Materialism: Believing that only material things matter and that there is no higher spiritual truth.
- Denial of the Divine: Thinking that there's no divine power or higher purpose in life.
- Insatiable Desires: Always wanting more and never being satisfied.
- Hypocrisy, Pride, and Arrogance: Pretending to be good or spiritual while secretly being proud and arrogant.
- Evil Ideas: Acting based on wrong or harmful thoughts.
- Unjust Means: Using unfair or dishonest ways to get what you want.
- Hatred for the Divine: Rejecting or hating the divine presence within yourself and others.

Anant: That sounds like a path to misery.

Kapil: Exactly. Following the asuri sampat qualities leads to destruction, not just of the soul but of our peace and happiness. Krishna says that there are three main gates to destruction: lust, anger, and greed. These three qualities are like doors to misery and suffering.

Anant: What should we do about those three gates?

Kapil: Krishna advises us to **forsake lust, anger, and greed**. If we free ourselves from these three dark qualities, we can practice what is good for us and reach the highest level of existence.

Those who are free from lust, anger, and greed live a life filled with peace, joy, and spiritual growth.

Anant: So, avoiding lust, anger, and greed is the key to staying on the right path?

Kapil: Yes, by getting rid of these negative qualities, we not only avoid suffering but also create the space for all the good qualities to grow. It's like clearing weeds in a garden so the flowers can bloom.

Anant: It seems like everything we do, good or bad, takes us either closer to or further from the divine.

Kapil: That's right, Anant. Every action, thought, and choice we make affects which path we walk. By nurturing daivi sampat and avoiding asuri sampat, we make sure we're moving toward the divine and living in harmony with our true selves.

Anant: I see now. It's all about choosing the right qualities and being aware of what guides us.

Kapil: Exactly, Anant. The more aware we are, the easier it becomes to live a life filled with peace, purpose, and connection to the divine.

Mantra:

Samatvam Yoga Uccayte

Meaning: Staying calm and balanced is Yoga.

This mantra teaches that real yoga isn't just about doing poses but also about keeping your mind calm and peaceful. When you can stay balanced, no matter what's happening—whether you're happy, sad, or even angry—you are practicing yoga in its truest form.

Gyan:

Which quality of Asuri sampat leads to destruction, as per Krishna's teaching?
a) Greed
b) Fortitude
c) Purity
d) Non-injury

What are the three main gates to destruction mentioned by Krishna?
a) Lust, Ignorance, and Anger
b) Lust, Anger, and Greed
c) Hypocrisy, Pride, and Anger
d) Hatred, Arrogance, and Desire

Answers: A, B

Karm: Connect the Dots: Path to the Divine

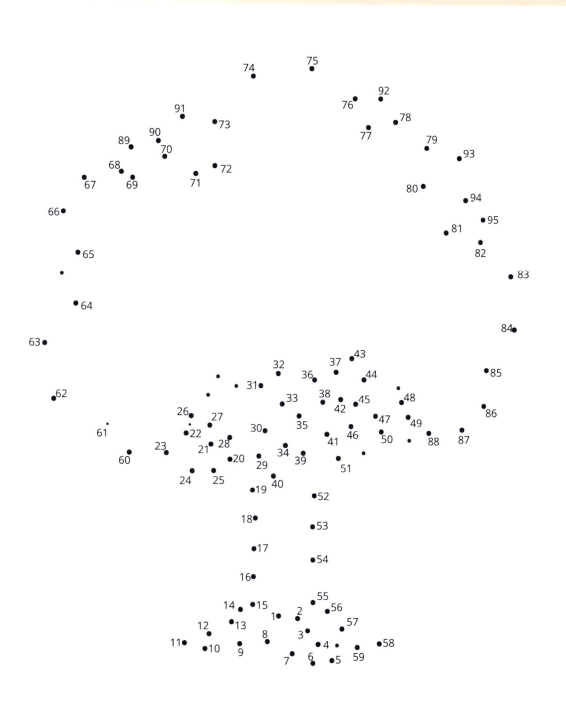

Chapter 28: Understanding the Influence of the Sastras and the Three Gunas

Anant: Kapil, we've talked about dharma and doing the right thing, but how do we know exactly what's right and wrong in every situation?

Kapil: That's a great question, Anant. To know what is right and wrong, we depend on the sastras. Sastras are the ancient scriptures or sciences that guide us in how we should live. Just like how physical science tells us about the natural world, spiritual science or sastras help us understand how to live a good life, both spiritually and physically. They teach us the rules and principles that are based on wisdom from the past, showing us the right path in our behaviors and actions.

Anant: So, sastras are like a guidebook for life?

Kapil: Exactly. They help us know what actions to take, how to treat others, and even how to manage our thoughts and feelings. But it's important to remember that the mind is influenced by three qualities: **Sattva, Rajas, and Tamas.**

Anant: We have discussed these at length before. Just to revise Kapil, can you explain what these qualities are, and how they affect us?

Kapil: The gunas are the forces that influence our behavior and thoughts:

- Sattva is the quality of goodness, light, and purity. A person with a sattvik mind will have good intentions and perform good actions.
- Rajas is about passion and energy. It often leads to desire and restlessness.
- Tamas is related to darkness, laziness, and ignorance. It clouds our judgment and causes inaction.

It's not just the actions that matter, but the state of the mind that drives those actions. So, instead of focusing only on what you do, work on your mind—make it more sattvik.

Anant: How do we know what a sattvik, rajasik, or tamasik mind prefers?

Kapil: Good question! Even the types of food you choose reflect your mind's nature. A sattvik mind prefers foods that give energy, health, strength, and happiness. These are fresh, nourishing foods like fruits, vegetables, grains, and dairy.

Anant: So, healthy, natural foods?

Kapil: Yes, exactly! On the other hand, a rajasik mind prefers spicy, bitter, or very hot foods. These foods can create restlessness and discomfort, like junk food or overly spicy dishes. While they may taste good, they often cause pain or illness in the long run.

MCQ

What are the Sastras?

A. Laws of the country

B. Ancient scriptures that guide us on how to live

C. Books about modern science

D. Instructions for performing rituals

2. Which guna is associated with goodness, light, and purity?

A. Rajas

B. Sattva

C. Tamas

D. Karma

3. What type of food does a sattvik mind prefer?

A. Spicy, hot foods

B. Stale, tasteless food

C. Fresh, nourishing food like fruits and vegetables

D. Junk food

Answers: B, B, C

Finally, a tamasik mind prefers foods that are stale, tasteless, or impure. This includes foods that have been left out overnight, or food that is unhealthy and not fresh. This type of food clouds the mind, making it difficult to think clearly or be active.

Anant: It seems like everything we do, even what we eat, can affect our mind. What about other habits like discipline? Does that matter too?

Kapil: Absolutely, and this is where the concept of tapas comes in. Tapas means self-discipline or austerity. There are three kinds of tapas—of the body, speech, and mind.

- Tapas of the body includes worship of the divine, respecting teachers and wise people, maintaining purity, and practicing non-violence.
- Tapas of speech means speaking truthfully, kindly, and in a way that is helpful and not hurtful. It also includes regularly studying sacred texts.
- Tapas of the mind involves keeping a peaceful and calm mind, being kind, controlling your thoughts, and always having good intentions.

When these forms of tapas are practiced with sincerity and without expecting anything in return, they are called sattvik tapas.

Anant: What about the other types of tapas?

Kapil: If tapas is practiced to gain attention, honor, or to show off, it becomes rajasik tapas. It's done for selfish reasons.

On the other hand, if someone uses tapas to hurt themselves or others, it's called tamasik tapas. This type of discipline is harmful and not true to the spirit of tapas.

Anant: So tapas isn't just about being strict or tough on yourself, but it's about doing it for the right reasons?

Kapil: Exactly, Anant. It's about self-improvement, not for praise or to harm others.

Anant: I've also heard about giving gifts in a selfless way. How does that relate to tapas?

Kapil: Giving is a form of self-discipline too. There are three types of gifts:
- A sattvik gift is given with no expectation of something in return. It's offered to a deserving person, at the right time, with a pure heart.
- A rajasik gift is given with the hope of getting something back, or with a selfish motive. The giver is thinking, "What's in it for me?"
- A tamasik gift is given without care or respect, at the wrong time or place, or to someone unworthy. It's given with disdain or with bad intentions.

Anant: It seems like everything—from how we act, to what we eat, say, think, and give—is influenced by the gunas.

Kapil: That's right. By focusing on cultivating more sattva in our lives, whether through food, actions, speech, or giving, we bring ourselves closer to peace, wisdom, and true happiness.

Anant: I'll definitely try to remember that and make better choices in all these areas!

Mantra:

Sarva Karma Phala Tyaga

Meaning: Imagine you work really hard on something—like a school project or helping someone at home. You naturally expect praise, good marks, or something in return, right? But Sarva Karma Phala Tyaga teaches us that we should do our work without worrying about the results. It means giving up the attachment to the outcome of our actions.

In simpler words: Do your best, but don't stress about what you will get in return. The goal is to focus on the action itself, and not be overly attached to rewards, praise, or results. When we let go of this attachment, we feel more peaceful and happy, because we aren't disappointed if things don't go exactly as we hoped.

So, keep doing your good work, whether you get a reward or not!

Did you know?

Colors can affect our emotions and mental states. Bright, light colors (associated with Sattva) can evoke feelings of happiness and calmness, while dark or muted colors (linked with Tamas) can induce feelings of sadness or lethargy

Gyan:

A rajasik mind prefers which type of food?

A. Stale, tasteless food

B. Fresh and natural food

C. Spicy, bitter, or very hot food

D. Sweet and mild food

What is the characteristic of a tamasik gift?

A. Given selflessly with no expectation of return

B. Given with selfish motives

C. Given without care or respect, to someone unworthy

D. Given at the right time with a pure heart

Answer: C, C

Karm: Situations

Read the following everyday situations. Think about the actions of the people involved. Which of the three gunas—Sattva (goodness and purity), Rajas (passion and restlessness), or Tamas (ignorance and laziness)—do you think is most dominant in each scenario? Write down your answer and explain why.

Example Scenarios:

Situation 1:

Riya chooses to spend her afternoon helping her younger sibling with homework.

Which guna is influencing her action?

Situation 2:

Arjun eats a large bag of chips and feels restless afterward.

Which guna is influencing his action?

Situation 3:

Maya leaves her room messy and stays in bed all day.

Which guna is influencing her action?

Chapter 29: The Path of True Renunciation

Anant: Kapil, what does it mean to renounce things? Do we stop doing everything?

Kapil: That's a great question, Anant. Renunciation doesn't mean giving up action. Instead, it means giving up the results or fruits of our actions. We still keep working, but we stop worrying about what we will get in return. This is called Tyaga—renunciation of the attachment to the results of our actions.
Anant: How do we give up attachment to the results?

Kapil: There are two main ways:
1. Bhakti: We can dedicate the fruits of our actions to the Divine. It's like saying, "I do this work for you, not for my own gain."
2. Jnana: This means understanding through knowledge that the results don't matter because we are only doing our duty. When we know that, we can let go of the attachment to outcomes.

Anant: What about things like yajna, dana, and tapas? Should we give those up too?

Kapil: No, we should never give those up. Yajna (sacrifice), Dana (charity), and Tapas (self-discipline) are important because they help to purify our minds. But even when we perform these, we should do them without attachment.

Anant: So, is there a wrong way to give things up?

Kapil: Yes, there are different types of tyaga (renunciation), and not all are good:

- Tamasik Tyaga: This is when someone gives up doing what they should out of laziness or fear. They think, "This is too hard, I don't want to do it," and they quit. That's not a good way.
- Rajasik Tyaga: This happens when someone gives up work because they think it's too much trouble. They give up out of frustration or selfishness, still thinking about themselves.
- Sattvik Tyaga: This is the best type of renunciation. In this, a person continues to do their duty but gives up the attachment to the action and the results. They do the work without hating the hard parts or clinging to the pleasant parts.

Anant: So, we should aim for sattvik tyaga, right? What about knowledge—does it work the same way?

Kapil: Yes, knowledge also has different levels:

- Sattvik Jnana: This is the understanding that behind all the differences we see, like you and me being separate people, there is one truth. We are both the same atman (soul) inside. Everything is connected.
- Rajasik Jnana: This kind of knowledge sees only the differences—like thinking that everyone is separate and there is no deeper connection.

MCQ

Which of the following describes Bhakti in relation to renunciation?

a) Giving up actions entirely

b) Dedicating the fruits of one's actions to the Divine

c) Ignoring the consequences of actions

d) Expecting rewards for good deeds

Which type of Tyaga involves giving up actions due to laziness or fear?

a) Rajasik Tyaga

b) Sattvik Tyaga

c) Tamasik Tyaga

d) None of the above

Answer: B, C

Did you know?

The Gita is originally written in Sanskrit, one of the oldest languages in the world, known for its intricate grammatical structure and poetic qualities, making it a rich source for linguistic studies.

- **Tamasik Jnana:** This is very limited knowledge, only seeing one thing and not understanding the bigger picture. It's like focusing on small details without understanding the truth behind them.

Anant: Does this apply to other things in life too?

Kapil: Yes, absolutely! The three gunas—sattva, rajas, and tamas—affect everything, including our actions, intellect, willpower, and even our happiness. Everything in the world is touched by these gunas.

Anant: Is it possible to go beyond these gunas?

Kapil: Yes! When we go beyond the gunas, we return to our original state, which is the Atman—our purest, highest self. But while we are living in this world, we can understand the gunas and use them wisely.

Anant: How can we change the gunas?

Kapil: We can adjust the gunas in ourselves through our actions and choices. If you notice that you are in a tamasik state, feeling lazy or confused, you can start by doing something to bring in rajasik energy—like being more active. Then, by making wise choices, you can move toward a sattvik state, where you feel peaceful and clear.

Anant: That sounds like it takes practice.

Kapil: It does, but it's worth it. When we achieve union with the Divine, we rise above all difficulties. Through the grace of the Divine, we find peace and freedom.

Anant: How do we know what path to take?

Kapil: Krishna explained this to Arjuna at the end of the Gita to help Arjuna resolve his dilemma whether to fight in the battle or not. He said, "I have given you the light of knowledge. Now, think it over and decide your own course of action." It's important to reflect on the wisdom we receive and make our own decisions.

Anant: And how did Arjuna respond?

Kapil: Arjuna said, "My doubts are gone, and my mind is steady now. I understand, and I will follow your guidance."

Anant: So, we should trust our learning of the Gita and act with confidence, right?

Kapil: Exactly. When we act with faith and wisdom, letting go of attachments, we find our true path and peace.

Mantra

Sarva Bhuta Hite Ratah

This mantra teaches us that we should try to care for and be kind to all living things—people, animals, plants—because they are all part of this big, beautiful world. When we act with kindness, not just thinking of ourselves but thinking of others too, we are following this idea of Sarva Bhuta Hite Ratah.

Gyan

What is the best way to move from a Tamasik to a Sattvik state?
a) By practicing inaction
b) By indulging in rajasik actions
c) By taking positive, active steps and making wise choices
d) By avoiding any type of action

Sattvik Jnana (knowledge) is defined as:
a) Seeing only differences between people
b) Understanding the unity behind all differences
c) Focusing only on material gains
d) Ignoring the spiritual aspects of life

Answers: C, B

Karm: Letting Go of Results

Draw whatever comes to your mind. Focus only on the act of drawing—how it feels to move the pencil or crayon across the paper. Don't worry about how the drawing will look when you're done. Let go of any thoughts about whether it's "good" or "bad."

This exercise helps you practice Sattvik Tyaga—letting go of attachment to the results of your actions.

Chapter 30: Resolving the Dilemma with Wisdom from the Gita

Kapil: Anant, it seems we've come to the end of our discussions. Over the past few weeks, we've explored the teachings of the Bhagavad Gita together, from understanding dharma and karma to seeing the deeper truths of life through jnana (knowledge). With this wisdom, do you feel more prepared to address the dilemma you've been facing? Do you feel clearer about what action to take?

Anant: Yes, Kapil, I do. After reflecting on everything we've discussed, I'm finally able to see my path forward. My mind was clouded by worry and fear before—worry about losing my friends and fear of the consequences if I act. But I've learned through the Gita that it's not the outcome of my actions that matters. What matters is doing the right thing, regardless of what happens afterward. It's my duty, my dharma, to protect that younger student, even if my friends might not like me for it.

Kapil: That's an important realization, Anant. Krishna explained to Arjuna that one must never shy away from performing one's duty, no matter how challenging it might seem. We must act in accordance with dharma, and leave the fruits of those actions to the divine.

Anant: Yes, and I realize now that my confusion was because I was too focused on the results—whether my friends would be punished, whether I would lose them. But as you taught me, through the Gita, I need to practice sarva karma phala tyaga—renouncing the fruits of my actions. What happens to my friends after I speak up is not something I can control, and it shouldn't stop me from doing what's right.

Kapil: Exactly. When you act with tyaga, renouncing attachment to the outcomes, your actions become purified. You act out of the right intention, not for personal gain or avoidance of pain. Krishna called this the path of nishkama karma—selfless action, performed without desire for the results. This is the foundation of a sattvik (pure) life.

Anant: I can see that now. Before, I thought I had to choose between helping the younger student or keeping my friends. But I understand that it's not about choosing sides. It's about standing for what is right. The Gita taught me that real strength comes from following dharma, even if it feels uncomfortable or difficult. If I stay silent, I'm allowing injustice to happen, and that's not something I can live with.

Kapil: Yes, Anant. By choosing the path of dharma, you're not just helping the younger student—you're also helping your friends. They might not realize it yet, but by allowing them to continue bullying, you're letting them harm themselves as well. When you stand up for what's right, you're guiding them toward a better path, even if they don't see it immediately.

Anant: That's true. And I remember when we discussed sarva bhuta hite ratah, the importance of dedicating oneself to the welfare of all beings. This situation is about more than just me or my friends. It's about the well-being of everyone involved. If I stay silent, I'm not helping anyone. But if I speak up, I'm acting for the good of all—protecting the younger student and giving my friends a chance to change.

Kapil: Well said, Anant. The Gita teaches us to act with compassion, even when others are not ready to see the truth. Your duty is to help your friends see the harm they are causing, and to protect those who are vulnerable. This is the essence of ahimsa—non-violence. It's not just about refraining from physical harm, but also standing against harm when you see it.

Anant: Yes, Kapil. I now realize that I can approach this situation with both firmness and compassion. I don't need to be angry or resentful toward my friends. Instead, I can take action with a clear heart, knowing that I'm acting out of love and a sense of duty. The Gita taught me that it's possible to be strong and gentle at the same time.

Kapil: That balance is key, Anant. Krishna taught Arjuna that samatvam yoga uccayate—true yoga is maintaining balance, regardless of success or failure, pleasure or pain. You must act with steadiness, without being swayed by attachment or aversion. Whether your friends appreciate your actions or not, you should continue to act with a calm and clear mind, rooted in dharma.

MCQ

What does Anant realize about his duty in the situation with the younger student?

A) He should prioritize his friendships above all else.

B) He must protect the younger student regardless of the consequences.

C) He should ignore the situation and focus on himself.

D) He should speak up only if his friends agree.

What does the term "sarva karma phala tyaga" refer to?

A) Renouncing all actions

B) Renouncing attachment to the results of actions

C) Seeking rewards for good deeds

D) Avoiding responsibilities

What is the concept of "nishkama karma"?

A) Selfless action without desire for the results

B) Actions performed for personal gain

C) Avoiding difficult tasks

D) Taking actions based on fear

Answers: B, B, A

Anant: I understand now, Kapil. I've learned that it's not about trying to control the outcome, but about controlling my own response to the situation. I need to stay calm, focused, and compassionate, even if things don't go as I hope. I'll speak to my teacher about the bullying, not out of a desire to punish my friends, but to protect the younger student and help everyone involved grow.

Kapil: You've grasped the essence of karma yoga, Anant. You're now ready to act without attachment, with compassion for all, and with a deep understanding of your dharma. This is the wisdom that Krishna gave to Arjuna in his moment of doubt. And now, like Arjuna, you've found clarity in your own path.

Anant: Yes, Kapil. The Gita has taught me that true strength comes from understanding, not from fear or attachment. I know what I need to do now. I'll approach my teacher and explain the situation, with a pure heart and the intention to help. I'm no longer afraid of the consequences because I'm acting with the right intention.

Kapil: That's the power of jnana—knowledge. When you see the world clearly, without the distortions of fear, attachment, or anger, you can act with confidence and peace. Krishna told Arjuna that once you understand the deeper truths of life, all doubts dissolve. And I can see that in you now, Anant.

Anant: Thank you, Kapil. My doubts are gone, and I feel a deep sense of peace. I no longer feel torn between conflicting desires.

I understand now that doing the right thing is not about the outcome—it's about the action itself. I'm ready to act, with compassion for my friends, the younger student, and myself.

Kapil: I'm proud of you, Anant. You've learned well. You've understood the teachings of the Gita and are ready to apply them in your life. This is the true test of wisdom—not just knowing the right thing, but having the courage to act on it. Go forward with confidence, knowing that you are guided by the light of dharma.

Anant: I will, Kapil. Thank you for all your guidance and wisdom. I feel lighter, clearer, and ready to face whatever comes next. No matter what happens, I know I'm doing the right thing. That's all that matters.

Mantra:

Etat Satyam, Tat Satyasya Satyam

Meaning: This is the truth, that is the truth of the truth.

This mantra is teaching us that we should live truthfully in our actions, and also remember that there is a deeper, ultimate truth guiding everything. It's like understanding that we are all connected by something greater, even if we can't always see it.

Gyan

What realization does Anant come to about his own strength?
A) Strength comes from controlling others.
B) True strength comes from following dharma, not from fear.
C) Strength is about being loud and forceful.
D) Strength means avoiding conflicts entirely.

What is the meaning of "samatvam yoga uccayate"?
A) True yoga is about pleasure and pain.
B) True yoga is maintaining balance in all circumstances.
C) True yoga is about competing with others.
D) True yoga requires isolation from society.

Answers: B, B

Karm: Dharma Wheel

Draw a large wheel divided into sections representing different aspects of your life (e.g., family, friends, school, self). In each section, write down your duties (dharma) related to that aspect and how you can fulfill them.

Made in United States
Troutdale, OR
04/17/2025

30691197R00159